100 AMERICANS

Who Shaped American History

Samuel Willard Crompton

A Bluewood Book

This edition produced and published
in 1999 by Bluewood Books
A Division of The Siyeh Group, Inc.,
P.O. Box 689
San Mateo, CA 94401

ISBN 0-912517-32-8

Printed in U.S.A.
10, 9, 8, 7, 6, 5, 4, 3

Edited by Lee A. Schoenbart
and Heidi Marschner
Copy Edited by Greg Aaron
Designed by David Price
Proofread by Gerry Hall

Key to cover illustration:
    Clockwise, starting from top left:
Betty Friedan, Paul Revere,
Benjamin Franklin, Ray Kroc, Eleanor
Roosevelt, Chief Joseph, Abraham
Lincoln, and George Washington in
the center.

About the Author:
    Samuel Willard Crompton
teaches American and European
history at Holyoke Community College.
Crompton's other books include: *100
Military Leaders Who Shaped World
History* (Bluewood, 1999), *100 Battles
That Shaped World History* (Bluewood,
1997), *100 Wars That Shaped World
History* (Bluewood, 1997), *Gods and
Goddesses of Classical Mythology*
(Barnes and Noble, 1998) and
Presidents of the United States
(Smithmark, 1992)
    Crompton holds degrees from
Framingham State College and Duke
University. He grew up and lives in
western Massachusetts.

Picture Acknowledgements: Apple
Computer Corp.:106; Bluewood
Archives: 13, 15, 16, 19, 21, 105;
Brigham Young University: 76;
California Dept. of Parks & Recreation:
45; Tony Chikes: 42, 83, 85, 100;
Columbia Broadcasting System: 92;
Columbia University: 66; Paul Farber,
courtesy of Dramatists Play Service:
86; Ford Motor Company: 68; FDR
Library: 77; The Hearst Corporation:
69; IBM Archive: 97; Levittown Public
Library: 91; Library of Congress: 8, 9,
10, 11, 12, 18, 20, 22, 23, 24, 25,
26, 28, 32, 33, 34, 36, 37, 38, 39,
48, 49, 51, 52, 54, 55, 56, 57, 58,
59, 61, 62, 63, 64, 65, 67, 70, 71,
73, 81, 84, 88, 89, 90, 94, 95, 96,
101, 102, 103; McDonald's Corporation: 87; Microsoft Corporation: 107;
National Archives: 14, 17, 27, 29,
30, 31, 35, 40, 41, 43, 44, 46, 47,
50, 53, 74, 75, 78, 79, 80, 82, 93,
99; NASA: 104; National Library of
Medicine: 98; University of South
Dakota: 60; U.S. Postal Service: 72.

2

TABLE OF CONTENTS

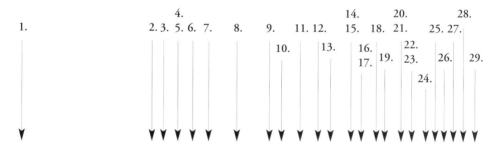

1700   1800

TABLE OF CONTENTS

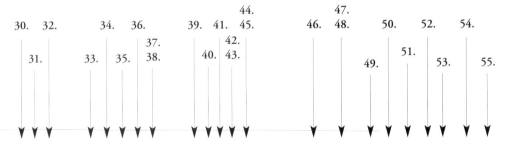

TABLE OF CONTENTS

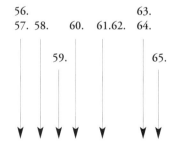

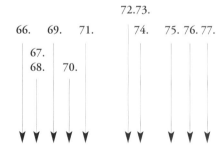

1851

1900

TABLE OF CONTENTS

79.80.81.

88. 90.

78.   82. 83.   89. 91.   92.   94.   95.   96.   98.   99.   100.

85.86.87.
84.

93.

97.

1901   **1955**

INTRODUCTION

Narrowing this collection to 100 men and women has been a difficult task. There are so many Americans, in so many fields of endeavor, who deserve recognition. The starting point was clearly drawn. Benjamin Franklin, whose life and career come close to approximating the American ideal of individual self-sufficiency, was born two generations removed from Europe.

Let us turn to the words of J. Hector St. John de Crevecoeur to consider what it meant to be an American during the late 18th century:

"What then is the American, this new man? ... I could point out to you a family whose grandfather was an Englishman, whose wife was Dutch, whose son married a French woman, and whose present four sons have now four wives of different nations. *He* is an American, who, leaving behind him all his ancient prejudices and manners, receives new ones from the new mode of life he has embraced, the new government he obeys, and the new rank he holds. He becomes an American by being received in the broad lap of our great Alma Mater. Here individuals of all nations are melted into a new race of men, whose labours and posterity will one day cause great changes in the world. Americans are the western pilgrims who are carrying along with them the great mass of arts, sciences, vigour, and industry which began long since in the east; they will finish, the great circle" (Crevecoeur, *Letters from an American Farmer*, 1782).

Arts, sciences, vigor and industry. Can any neutral observer deny that Americans have often led the way in these and other fields of endeavor?

From Franklin, who first experimented with electricity, to Bill Gates, who revolutionized the computer industry, Americans have consistently seized the moment and pushed forward the arts in a practical manner. Robert Fulton pioneered in the scientific arena with his relentless desire to produce a steamboat. In more recent times J. Robert Oppenheimer left no stone unturned in his desire to unearth the secrets of nuclear energy.

If "vigor" can be applied to the jack-of-all-trades approach to life, then surely Susan B. Anthony, P. T. Barnum, Davy Crockett and Mary Baker Eddy can be said to represent a uniquely American type of vigor.

In the scope of industry, Americans have consistently led the way, from Eli Whitney's cotton gin to Henry Ford's Model T car to William Levitt's mass construction of homes. Finally, by adding the category of politics, we can point to innovative leaders such as Andrew Jackson, Theodore Roosevelt and Franklin D. Roosevelt, as well as many beloved Americans who never reached the high offices they aspired to, such as Daniel Webster, Henry Clay and William Jennings Bryan.

How did Crevecoeur so clearly foresee this trait that would prove to define Americans? What indicated to him the peculiar American spirit that has carried its energy so far? We might conjecture he saw the American attitudes of eagerness, impatience and diligence as well as that singularly American approach to history as a type of "manifest destiny."

The 100 Americans presented here are individuals who, added together, provide examples of the American spirit. They are indeed Americans who were conscious of, and appreciated, their earlier cultural heritage. They are Americans who seized opportunities and pressed forward with new ideas, inventions, religious systems and business innovations. These are the pilgrims whose spirit invigorated American life, and with their courage and determination, brought greatness to their country.

1. Benjamin Franklin
(1706–1790)

The most famous American of his time, **Benjamin Franklin** was born in Boston, Massachusetts. The 15th child of 17, he went to work in his father's candle shop and then in the print shop owned by his older half-brother, James. After quarreling with his brother and feeling a need to establish himself on his own terms, he departed for Philadelphia, Pennsylvania, in 1723.

Franklin rose from impoverishment to become owner of his own newspaper and print shop in 1730, the same year that he married. He published a periodical called *Poor Richard's Almanack* from 1732–1757; it dispensed witticisms and proverbs such as "Eat to live, don't live to eat," as well as practical advice on farming and the merchant trade. By 1748, Franklin had succeeded to the point where he could go into semi-retirement.

Franklin then turned to experiments with science, especially electricity, which occupied his time for several years. Franklin conducted experiments on electricity in a laboratory set up in his house and published a book on his findings that became widely read by other scientists. He also invented a more efficient stove that quickly became popular in his day and is still in wide use today. Also, during this time, Franklin was very active in civic affairs.

He helped establish the first circulating library in America as well as the first volunteer fire company and the first hospital. Then, in 1753, he was appointed deputy postmaster general of the American colonies. In 1751, Franklin made his entry into local politics. He went to England in 1757 and remained there as the agent for Pennsylvania and then for Massachusetts until 1775. As a government agent, he defended the colonists during the **Stamp Act** controversy in 1765. Thanks in part to his efforts, the act was repealed.

By the time he returned to Philadelphia in 1775, Franklin had become a confirmed

Benjamin Franklin

patriot. He served in the Second Continental Congress and was a member of the four-person committee that drafted the **Declaration of Independence**, which he signed at age 70.

In 1787, though so sick and aged he could hardly stand, he served as a member of the Constitutional Convention that drafted the new **United States Constitution**. He died in Philadelphia on April 17, 1790. His funeral was attended by some 20,000 persons. His remarkable life had spanned three crucial generations of American history, and at the time of his death he was the American most admired both at home and abroad, second only to George Washington.

2. George Washington
(1732–1799)

Born in Westmoreland County, Virginia, **George Washington** grew up in comfortable circumstances, although he had to shoulder much family responsibility due to the early death of his father. From an early age he exhibited high standards of honesty, integrity and courage.

After working as a surveyor, he entered the Virginia colonial militia and led his men in a skirmish in western Pennsylvania that preceded the **French and Indian War** in 1754. The next year he led colonial American troops in a battle known as "Braddock's Defeat," followed by the defense of the Virginia frontier against French and Indian raids.

When the war ended, Washington returned home. On January 6, 1759, he married Martha Dandridge Custis, Virginia's wealthiest widow. Washington lived the genteel life of a plantation farmer in Virginia between 1760 and 1775, which included service in the Virginia House of Burgesses.

When the **American Revolution** broke out in 1775, he was named by the Second Continental Congress as commander-in-chief of the American forces. He went north to Boston, Massachusetts and assumed command of the troops in July 1775. He found an unwieldy collection of militia bands recruited from various colonies and, through willpower and perseverance, turned them into a true Continental Army. He won three of the most dramatic battles of the war (**Trenton, Princeton** and the **Siege of Yorktown**). When the war ended in 1783, he was the single most admired man in North America.

Following a brief four years of semi-retirement at **Mount Vernon**, Washington served as leader of the Constitutional Convention (1787). Elected as the **first president of the United States**, he was inaugurated on April 30, 1789, and served for two four-year terms as chief executive. Keenly aware of the impor-

tance of precedent, he sought always to convey a sense of dignity and authority to the office he held. Horrified by the thought of political factions, he tried to balance his Cabinet, employing the liberal **Thomas Jefferson** (see no. 8) as secretary of state and the conservative **Alexander Hamilton** (see no. 12) as secretary of the treasury. The infighting between the two men — which Washington deplored — foreshadowed the beginning of party politics in America.

Prior to his leaving office in March 1797 (he refused a third nomination to the presidency), Washington issued a farewell address in which he urged Americans to avoid political factions and foreign entanglements. He retired to Mount Vernon, and spent a pleasant two years there before his death. As the 18th century ended, Washington received accolades and obituaries from around the world.

George Washington

3. Daniel Boone
(1734–1820)

The archetypal American frontiersman, **Daniel Boone,** was born in 1734 near Reading, Pennsylvania to Quaker parents. As a youth, Boone helped his father in the family businesses of weaving, blacksmithing and stock raising. By the age of 12, Daniel showed he truly aspired to be a hunter. The Boone family moved to North Carolina in 1751. Boone served as a teamster and blacksmith with British general **Edward Braddock**'s expedition, which was ambushed by the French and Indians in western Pennsylvania in 1755. On that campaign, Boone met John Finley, a veteran hunter and frontiersman, who told him of the land known as Kentucky, beyond the Appalachian Mountains.

He made his first trip into Kentucky in 1767–1768. From 1769 to 1771, he led a small group of explorers who made their way through the **Cumberland Gap** and reached

Daniel Boone

present-day Estill County, Kentucky. Returning to North Carolina, Boone joined the Transylvania Company in organizing a large group of settlers. In March 1775 (just one month before the start of the American Revolution), he led them down the **Wilderness Road** to the site that would become **Boonesborough**, Kentucky**.**

The start of the **Revolutionary War** made life even more hazardous for American settlers in Appalachia. Boone himself was captured by **Shawnee Indians** in February 1778, but escaped in June of that year and led an inspired defense of Boonesborough against the Indians.

Boone moved to Maysville, Kentucky in 1786. Disappointed in his attempts to gain government recognition of his landholding, he left Kentucky and went to present-day West Virginia in 1788. Foremost among the explorers and settlers of his time, he could not secure title to lands and therefore was forced to keep moving in search of new areas. From 1798 to 1799, he moved with his family to present-day Missouri. Boone served as magistrate of the district from 1800 until his death.

Boone returned to Kentucky only once, in 1810, to repay his debts. This was a tremendous accomplishment and gave him a sense of satisfaction, although it was rumored the accounting had left him with a surplus of only 50 cents! He traversed the Appalachian Mountains, brought American settlers to Kentucky, and set a pattern of exploration and settlement that became the model for the next two generations. Like many frontier heroes, he lived by his wits, improvised where he could, and ended up with little more than his reputation. Chester Harding, a portrait painter, met and painted Boone shortly before the frontiersman's death; it is probably the only accurate likeness that survives Boone.

4. John Adams
(1735–1826)

The second president of the United States, **John Adams** was born in Braintree, Massachusetts. He graduated from Harvard College in 1755, was admitted to the bar in 1758 and began to practice law.

Adams defended Boston merchant **John Hancock** (see no. 7) in the trial regarding Hancock's ship *Liberty*. Firmly within the patriot camp by 1770, Adams surprised his fellow Bostonians when he stepped forward to serve as defense counsel for the British soldiers who had been indicted after the **Boston Massacre**. Having shown that he could be objective in the best traditions of Anglo-American justice, Adams continued to play a prominent role among the Boston patriots. One of the **Sons of Liberty**, he served in the First and Second Continental Congresses and was a member of the five-person committee selected to draft the **Declaration of Independence**.

Adams was president of the Board of War (1775–1777) before he went overseas to serve as minister to the Netherlands (1780–1782). Like **Ben Franklin** (see no. 1), he too, was one of the peace negotiators for the **Treaty of Paris** that ended the **Revolutionary War** in 1783. A truly personal triumph for Adams came in 1785 when he was welcomed by King **George III**, as the new American minister to Great Britain.

Adams was elected as the first vice president of the United States and served under **George Washington** (see no. 2). He then won the 1796 presidential election as the leader of the Federalist Party. As president (1797–1801), Adams was confronted by the possibility of war with America's former ally, France. Generally distrustful of the French, he became even more so after France rejected his proposals of negotiation in the infamous "**XYZ Affair**" of 1797 and 1798. Refusing to yield to the popular clamor for a full-scale

John Adams

war, Adams instead declared a limited naval war against France. The new American Navy was highly successful and the war ended with a treaty in 1800.

Following his loss to **Thomas Jefferson** (see no. 8), Adams retired to Massachusetts. One of his last acts as president was to appoint **John Marshall** (see no. 11) as chief justice of the United States. Adams left Washington in haste to avoid meeting with Jefferson; the two men had become bitter foes during the division into the Federalist and Democratic-Republican parties. Adams became reconciled to his former foe in their joint state of retirement around 1813. The two corresponded at length and came to a state of mutual admiration, although from afar. Adams died 50 years to the day since he and Jefferson signed the Declaration of Independence. Knowing this, Adams' last words were "Thomas Jefferson still lives." Ironically, Jefferson died that same day.

5. Paul Revere
(1735–1818)

Paul Revere

America's most famous messenger was born in Boston, Massachusetts to Apollos Revoire (a Huguenot who had escaped persecution in France) and Deborah Hitchbourne. **Paul Revere** (the name was changed to accommodate English-American culture) received a basic education in Boston schools and then worked in his father's silversmith trade. He saw his first military service in 1756, when he joined an expedition against Fort Crown Point in New York during the **French and Indian War.**

He set up his silversmith shop, became a Freemason, and came to associate with promi-

nent Bostonians such as **John Adams** (see no. 4), **Samuel Adams** and **Joseph Warren**. It is not certain when he became a confirmed patriot. However, in 1770, he did an engraving of the **Boston Massacre**, a picture that clearly showed his sympathies toward the growing cause of freedom for the colonies. After becoming a leader of the Boston **Sons of Liberty**, he participated in the **Boston Tea Party** and became a dispatch rider for the Boston Committee of Safety.

During 1774, Revere rode to Philadelphia, Pennsylvania and Portsmouth, New Hampshire on a number of important missions for the Committee of Safety. His most famous service, however, took place during the night hours of April 18–19, 1775. Having learned that British general **Thomas Gage** was sending a column of troops out of Boston to arrest Samuel Adams and **John Hancock** (see no. 7), as well as to confiscate the patriot stores of ammunition at Concord, Revere was sent by the Committee to warn of the British plan. After being rowed across the Charles River to Charlestown, he rode to Concord, possibly crying out "The British are coming!" to homes along his route. Revere never made it to Concord. He was detained by British patrols after he left Lexington. Dr. **Samuel Prescott** was the dispatch rider who reached and alerted the town of Concord. Nevertheless, Revere's ride was commemorated in **Henry Wadsworth Longfellow**'s poem in 1863, and became an important part of the mystique of the American Revolution.

He went back to silversmithing, designed the Massachusetts state seal and molded much of the hardware for the frigate *USS Constitution*. A Federalist in his politics, he wore the clothing typical of the Revolutionary era until his death; it had gone out of style 20 years earlier. He was buried in the Granary Burial Ground in Boston.

6. Patrick Henry
(1736–1799)

The firebrand of the Revolution was born in 1736 on a family plantation in Hanover County, Virginia. The second son in his family, **Patrick Henry** had little formal education. Only by turning to law did Henry find the right path for his talents and the prospect of success.

Admitted to the bar after having trained himself, Henry became a prominent attorney by 1763. Elected to the House of Burgesses in 1765, he arrived there in time to confront the **Stamp Act** — the first direct tax ever placed upon the colonies by England. Henry introduced seven resolutions that collectively aimed at resisting the tax, and he concluded his famous speech against the tax with the words, "If this be treason, make the most of it."

Having become a patriot early in his career, Henry was a delegate to the first, second and third Virginia conventions (1774–1776). He played a major role in drafting the new Virginia state constitution after the Revolution began, and served as the first governor of the new state (1776–1779). Following the death of his mentally ill wife, he married Dorothea Dandridge in 1777; the couple had 11 children. Henry resigned as governor in 1779 and stayed out of politics for several years. He returned to run for and win the gubernatorial position again in 1784 and served until 1786. By then, he was content to play the role of the retired patriot, but the advent of the **Constitutional Convention** in Philadelphia roused him from his fireside. He denounced the new United States **Constitution**, as written by the delegates in Philadelphia, asserting that it threatened the rights of both the people and the states of the new country. His virulent opposition to the document was largely responsible for the creation of the **Bill of Rights** (1791), which enshrined individual liberties.

Henry was offered the position of Secretary of State by **George Washington** (see no. 2) in 1795. He declined the offer while declaring his admiration for, and faith in, the president. He ran for, and won, election to the Virginia House of Delegates in 1799, but died of stomach cancer before he could be seated.

Apart from his speech about treason, Henry's most famous remarks were "I am not a Virginian, but an American" (1774) and "Give me liberty or give me death!" (The latter was delivered on March 23, 1775, at the Provincial Convention in Richmond, preparing the people for resistance.)

Patrick Henry

John Hancock
(1737–1793)

He was to become the richest Bostonian of his time, but **John Hancock** was born in Braintree, Massachusetts to an impoverished minister and his wife. After the death of his father, Hancock was adopted by his uncle, Thomas Hancock, the wealthiest merchant in Boston. John Hancock graduated from Harvard College in 1754 and immediately entered the Hancock mercantile business. In 1760, he went to London for a year to learn about the English side of the trade. At the age of 27, he inherited the business and a personal fortune of £70,000 pounds sterling upon the death of his uncle.

Hancock became affiliated with the patriot faction in Boston through the seizure of his sloop, *Liberty*, by British customs agents in 1768. The Boston populace found itself able to identify with the wealthy Hancock who lost his ship at the same time Boston became occupied by British troops. Hancock was elected to the Massachusetts General Court (1769) and led the Boston town committee the following year. During this time, he was influenced by **Samuel Adams**, who pushed his ideas farther in the direction of liberty and independence. Hancock married Dorothy Quincy in 1775.

When the General Court changed to a Provincial Congress in 1774, Hancock became its first president. He went as a delegate to the **Continental Congress** in 1775 and served as its president from 1775–1777. Hancock was the first person to sign the **Declaration of Independence** (July 4, 1776). He signed with an extravagant flourish typical of 18th century notables and declared "There! I guess King George will be able to read that!"

Hancock nourished even greater ambitions; he fancied himself a soldier and was bitterly disappointed when Congress selected **George Washington** (see no. 2) to be commander-in-chief of the army. After leaving the Continental Congress in 1777, Hancock transferred his interest to Massachusetts politics. He was a member of the constitutional convention that wrote the Massachusetts state constitution in 1780 and served as governor of the state from 1780–1785 and 1787–1793. He led the Massachusetts convention that ratified the federal **Constitution** in 1788, and died at the age of 56 while serving as governor. Hancock served an important function; his wealth and status combined with his revolutionary spirit illustrated that the Revolution could attract members of the patrician class in America.

John Hancock

8. Thomas Jefferson
(1743–1826)

During his life **Thomas Jefferson** became a near legend to many Americans who venerated his ideals of self-sufficiency and democratic government. Although the notions of **Alexander Hamilton** (strong federal government), (see no. 12) came to overshadow Jefferson's vision for America (strong state governments), it is Jefferson who remains admired to this day as spokesperson for the noble and simple expression of American values of rural life and self-sufficiency. The great contradiction inherent in Jefferson's life — his ideal of rural America was sustained by the system of African-American slavery.

He graduated from the College of William and Mary in 1762, having already exhibited extensive knowledge of Latin and Greek that would class him as perhaps the most learned American of his day.

Jefferson was elected to the Virginia House of Burgesses in 1769. Never a radical, he tilted slowly toward the view that the American colonies were oppressed by the taxes and laws of Great Britain. When the Revolutionary War began in 1775, he was ready to participate in what became the most celebrated event of his life — the writing of the **Declaration of Independence**. As leader of the five-person committee named by the Continental Congress to draft the document — **Benjamin Franklin**, **John Adams**, **Robert R. Livingston** and **Roger Sherman** were the others — Jefferson produced a masterpiece of erudition and expression. Beginning with his famous premise, "All men are created equal,"

Thomas Jefferson

stating men had an inalienable right to "life, liberty and the pursuit of happiness," Jefferson's words became the secular faith of an entire generation of American patriots.

He served as governor of Virginia (1779–1781) and represented the United States at the court of Louis XVI in France (1785–1789). In 1782, Jefferson returned to **Monticello**, his beloved estate. In 1789, he went to New York City to serve under George Washington as the first American Secretary of State. Following three exhausting years of feuding with Alexander Hamilton over the nation's direction, Jefferson resigned his post and returned to Virginia. Eventually, he went back to politics as vice president of the country (1797–1801).

Jefferson ran for and won the presidency in 1800. His two terms in office saw the acquisition of the **Louisiana Territory** from France, the first transcontinental journey by white men (**Lewis and Clark** [see no. 19]), and the first declared war of the United States (fought against the pirates of North Africa).

He returned to Monticello, continued to invent, and was content to live the life of a gentleman farmer. In 1813, he began to correspond with his old political foe, **John Adams** (see no. 4); the two patriots, in their old age, pondered the fate of liberty and democracy. A lifelong slave owner, Jefferson admitted he shuddered when he considered that slavery had increased in the United States during his lifetime. He died at Monticello, exactly 50 years to the day after signing the Declaration of Independence.

9. James Madison
(1751–1836)

James Madison was born in Port Conway, Virginia on a 5,000-acre, 100-slave plantation. A member of Virginia's colonial aristocracy, he went north to study and graduated from the College of New Jersey (later Princeton) in 1771. Attracted to the patriot cause from an early age, he served on the Orange County Committee of Safety (1774), was a delegate to the Virginia Convention (1776), and served in the new state legislature of Virginia (1776–1780; 1784–1786). He saw no active military service in the Revolutionary War, but was close to the scene of action in Virginia while serving on the governor's council (1777–1779).

As a member of the Virginia legislature, Madison called for the **Constitutional Convention** of 1787. One of 57 delegates to the convention, he argued in favor of a strong national government and was largely responsible for inserting the "checks and balances" structure (shared power among the executive, legislative and judicial branches) that is such an important part of American government. Madison's notes form the only complete record of the convention's proceedings, and his effect on the final document has led many scholars to call him "the father of the Constitution." Madison later co-wrote *The Federalist Papers* with **Alexander Hamilton** (see no. 12) and **John Jay**, defending the need for a strong federal government.

During the 1790s, Madison came to distrust the views of Alexander Hamilton and the wisdom of an excessively powerful federal government. He wrote the **Virginia Resolutions** to voice his opposition to the **Alien and Sedition Acts** of 1798. Having cast his lot with the Democratic-Republican Party, Madison served as Secretary of State from 1801 to 1809 under his former Virginia neighbor **Thomas Jefferson** (see no. 8). In 1808, he easily won both the Democratic-Republican nomination and the presidential election.

As president (1809–1817), Madison was unable to avoid the embroilment caused by the Napoleonic wars in Europe. Faced with impressment of American sailors into the British Army and a clamor for war by the newly elected "**War Hawks**" in Congress, Madison requested and was granted a declaration of war against Great Britain in June 1812. Madison's fortunes hit their lowest ebb in August 1814 when British troops descended on and burned parts of Washington, D.C. Madison and his wife rose superbly to the occasion. They returned quickly to the charred capital and insisted they would rebuild the city at once. American victories late in the war ensured it would end as a draw. The **Treaty of Ghent** in 1814 returned all the territory that had been taken by both sides.

Madison spent two final, triumphant years as president after the war ended. In 1817, he retired to his plantation amid a wave of popularity, and practiced scientific agriculture until his death.

James Madison

16

10. Betsy Ross
(1752–1836)

The controversy remains: did **Betsy Ross** of Philadelphia, Pennsylvania design the first flag of the United States? While little substantial evidence has come forth that she did, nothing proves that she did not. There is at least a full life story that can be sketched around what may or may not be fact.

Elizabeth Griscom was born in Philadelphia to Quaker parents in 1752. When she married John Ross, an Anglican, in 1773, she was disowned by her Quaker church for having married out of the faith.

She and her husband set up an upholstery and sewing business in Philadelphia. John Ross was fatally injured in a gunpowder explosion in January 1776, leaving Betsy a widow at 24.

She married Joseph Ashburn in 1777; the couple had two children before he was taken to England as a prisoner. Ashburn died in an English prison in 1782. A fellow prisoner, John Claypoole, gained his freedom and went to Philadelphia to deliver the news in person to Ross, now widowed for the second time.

In 1783, Betsy Ross married for the third and final time, to Claypoole; the couple had five daughters. Claypoole died in 1817, but Betsy Ross, three times a widow, lived to the age of 84. She ran the upholstery and sewing shop for more than 50 years.

In 1870, one of Betsy Ross' grandsons told a remarkable story to the Philadelphia Historical Society — his grandmother had been visited by **George Washington** (see no. 2), Robert Morris and George Ross in her shop in 1776, and was asked to create the first American flag. According to the story, she had suggested the use of the five-pointed star rather than six-pointed, as they were easier to sew. The periodical *Harper's Monthly* reported the story in 1873 and three years later, at the 100th anniversary of the Declaration of Independence, the story

Betsy Ross

became widespread and entered American folklore.

The only significant documentary evidence for this story is an invoice recorded by the Pennsylvania State Navy Board. Among its records was an invoice for 14 pounds, 12 shillings, 2 pence to Elizabeth Ross for making flags for ships.

Congress did create the American flag by resolution on June 14, 1777, but there is no record of who designed or sewed it. Since the matter has never been fully proved or disproved, there seems to be no harm in promoting Betsy Ross as the possible creator of the American flag, a modest woman who showed remarkable endurance and fortitude in her life.

11. John Marshall
(1755–1835)

John Marshall

Born in a log cabin in what is now Fauquier County, Virginia, **John Marshall** was a third cousin of **Thomas Jefferson** (see no. 8). An eager patriot, Marshall jumped at the chance to serve as an officer in the **American Revolution**. He fought in the battles of **Brandywine**, **Monmouth** and **Stony Point**, and was one of thousands of soldiers who endured the fierce winter of 1777–1778 at **Valley Forge**, Pennsylvania.

He was elected to the Virginia House of Delegates in 1782 and was instrumental in ratification of the U.S. Constitution at the Virginia Convention of 1788. Marshall served in the House until 1790, and reentered it from 1795–1796.

He declined an offer from President **George Washington** (see no. 2) to be Attorney General of the United States in 1795. He was one of three commissioners sent by President **John Adams** (see no. 4) to France in 1797. The American commissioners refused to pay a bribe to negotiate with French Foreign Minister **Talleyrand**. Marshall returned home to a warm welcome because of his rejection of the three French agents, known at the time only as "Messieurs X, Y and Z."

He served in the U.S. House of Representatives (1799–1800) and as Secretary of State (1800–1801). On January 20, 1801, President Adams named him Chief Justice of the United States. For the next 34 years, Marshall dominated the court in a way that no chief justice has since done.

Only two years after becoming chief justice, he was confronted by the momentous *Marbury v. Madison* case (1803), which challenged him to find a solution to the "midnight appointments" of President Adams. In a masterful sleight-of-hand, Marshall wrote the decision which allowed that commissions given by Adams did indeed have to be delivered, but he did so in a way that established "judicial review," that is, the right of the Supreme Court to review the constitutionality of all laws passed by Congress and signed by the president.

A confirmed Federalist, and a believer in central authority, Marshall made only one serious misstep in his years on the bench. In 1807, he appeared to take cause with defendant **Aaron Burr**, who was tried for treason. Seeing the flagrant attempt by President Jefferson to have Burr found guilty, Marshall made a strict interpretation of the definition of treason — and Burr walked out of the court a free man. In doing so, Marshall brought down the wrath of the Jeffersonians (who supported the president) and many Federalists, who remembered that Burr had shot and killed their hero, **Alexander Hamilton** (see no. 12), in a duel.

Marshall remained on the bench until his death, and the **Liberty Bell** in Philadelphia mysteriously cracked while ringing for his funeral. He was as important to the development of American law as George Washington had been to the establishment of American government.

12. Alexander Hamilton
(1757–1804)

One of the most ambitious and influential of the "founding fathers," **Alexander Hamilton** was born on the island of Nevis in the West Indies. The son of a Scottish merchant and a French woman, he went to work in a general store at the age of 12. Showing an early talent for languages and mathematics, he was sent to the mainland of North America to further his education. He arrived in New York City around 1773 and studied at King's College (later Columbia University).

Hamilton decided to join the patriot cause, and he became a captain of artillery in 1776. He received his baptism of fire at the battle of **Long Island** and served with distinction at both **Trenton** and **Princeton**. He became aide-de-camp to **George Washington** (see no. 2) in 1777, and the two men — very different in temperament and attitude — became close friends. Hamilton also fought at **Yorktown**, served briefly in the **Continental Congress** (1782–1783), practiced law in New York City, and was the founder of the Bank of New York (1784).

Hamilton was a member of the **Constitutional Convention** that wrote the new United States **Constitution** (1787), and he wrote numerous letters to the New York press in favor of ratification. These became known as *The Federalist Papers*. In 1789, President Washington named him the first Secretary of the Treasury.

Alexander Hamilton

Hamilton entered fully into his element while directing the nation's finances. He wrote the brilliant *Report on the Public Credit* (1790) and *Report on a National Bank* (1790), which contributed to creating the first permanent national financing system (as well as a substantial national debt).

He was the leader of the Federalist Party in the 1796 elections. In 1800, he urged his fellow Federalists to support Democratic-Republican **Thomas Jefferson** (see no. 8) for president rather than allow the unscrupulous **Aaron Burr** to win the presidency.

In 1804, Burr sought to win the governorship of New York State. After losing the election, he challenged Hamilton to a duel, based on Hamilton's published remarks about his character. Hamilton reluctantly agreed to the duel and on July 11, 1804, the two men met under the Weehawken heights on the New Jersey bank of the Hudson River. Hamilton did not take aim and the shot he fired into the air was harmless. Burr fired straight at his opponent and mortally wounded him.

Hamilton died the next day. His death did not erase the deep imprint he had left on American finances and government. Hamilton's vision of a powerful central government — strong enough to tax, regulate, create and enforce laws — has persisted.

13. **Noah Webster** (1758–1843)

Born in West Hartford, Connecticut in 1758, **Noah Webster** was the son of a dairy farmer. He entered Yale College in New Haven in 1774, just prior to the start of the **Revolutionary War**, and his college years were filled with irregularities and interruptions caused by the conflict. The school was briefly closed due to the need to conserve resources. He graduated with his B.A. degree from Yale in 1778 and proceeded to study the law. He passed the bar exam but chose to become a teacher instead of a lawyer.

In 1782, Webster began to write a series of elementary textbooks while teaching in Goshen, New York. It was the start of a long career as the premier American lexicographer. He came out with a speller in 1783, which had its name changed to *The American Spelling Book* in 1787. Part two of his *Grammatical Institution of the English Language* was a grammar text that was published in 1784 and revised in 1807 and 1831. The third element of his presentation was a reader in 1785.

By this time, Webster was well known to many American readers. He spent much of the late 1780s traveling the country and obtaining new source materials. He briefly edited the *American Magazine* (1787–1788) and then moved to Hartford, where he practiced law. In 1793, he was called to New York City by members of the Federalist Party who begged him to edit the daily *American Minerva* (1793–1798) and a semi-weekly, the *Herald*. He moved back to New Haven in 1798 and continued his studies of the varieties of the English language.

Webster published *A Compendious Dictionary of the English Language* in 1806 and *A Diet … for the Use of Common Schools* in 1807. He moved to Amherst, Massachusetts in 1812 where he participated in the founding of Amherst College. He returned to New Haven

Noah Webster

in 1822 and went abroad in 1824 to find new source materials and a new publisher for his last dictionary, which was finally coming to completion.

He finished the dictionary on English soil and labored in vain to find a British publisher. Returning to the United States, he published it himself. *An American Dictionary of the English Language* (1828), was his monumental and final work, with approximately 70,000 words — 12,000 more than **Samuel Johnson**'s famous English dictionary. Webster appeared to have proved his point: there was a distinct "American" brand of English, quite different from the one practiced in Great Britain. The diffident youth, the scribbler from Yale, had achieved his goal and declared America's cultural independence from England.

14. Robert Fulton
(1765–1815)

The man who proved the practicability of steamboat navigation was born in Little Britain, Lancaster County, Pennsylvania. **Robert Fulton** showed proficiency in drawing at an early age and designed a hand-propelled paddle-wheel boat. He went to Philadelphia at the age of 17 and supported himself for four years by drawing miniature portraits.

Leaving America for England in 1786, he probably had no idea that he would spend the next 30 years abroad. Fulton studied painting under **Benjamin West** (1738–1820) in London, and exhibited two portraits in 1791. Then he turned to the study of canals and locks. He obtained a British patent for a double inclined plane that could replace canal locks (1794), invented a digging machine, and wrote *A Treatise on the Improvement of Canal Navigation* (1796). Fulton sent copies to President **George Washington** (see no. 2), hoping to interest him in his ideas.

His scientific endeavors took him to France in 1797, where Fulton tried to interest the French government in a "plunging boat" that would enable the French to defeat the English at sea. He launched the *Nautilus* at Rouen in 1800; the twenty-four-and-a-half-foot ship stayed submerged for four hours while Fulton and others breathed air through a pump. Fulton then used the submarine to blow up a boat with clock-work mines, but the Napoleonic government was too conservative in mechanical matters to sponsor his work.

Fulton returned to England and replicated his experiments, but the English government would not finance his works, either.

Fortunately, Fulton made the acquaintance of **Robert R. Livingston** (1746–1813), who was then the American minister to France. Livingston had acquired a 20-year monopoly on steamboat navigation for New York State, and he was willing to finance Fulton's experiments. The two men launched an experimental steamboat on the Seine River in France in 1803.

Fulton returned to the United States where he designed and built the steamboat, *Clermont*. On August 17, 1807, the 133-by-18-foot boat left New York City's harbor under the power of its 15-foot side paddle wheels. The *Clermont* made the run up the Hudson River to Albany, New York in 33 hours, and the return voyage down river in 30 hours, demonstrating that steamboats could indeed serve a purpose. Regular sailing of the ship began in September 1807.

He went on to patent American steam engines (1809), and in 1814, was commissioned to build the *Demologus*, the first steam warship, to protect the harbor of New York. Fulton died knowing the product he had demonstrated was spreading to the Raritan, Potomac, Ohio and Mississippi rivers. Soon, the steamboat would revolutionize water transport in North America, allowing for rapid transit between towns as far apart as Pittsburgh, Pennsylvania and New Orleans, Louisiana.

Robert Fulton

Eli Whitney

The inventor who did the most to change the means of production in early 19th century America, **Eli Whitney** was born in Westboro, Massachusetts in 1765. Whitney showed mechanical ability at an early age, making nails at home by the age of 15. Eager to have a college education, he taught school in order to pay for his years at Yale College (1789–1792). He then moved to Savannah, Georgia in order to teach, but found on his arrival the position had been filled. Looking for stopgap work, he accepted the invitation of the widow of General **Nathanael Greene** (1742–1786) to stay on her plantation.

While at the Greenes, Whitney heard from a number of southern planters that their greatest difficulty was separating green seeds from short-staple cotton fiber. After pondering the matter, Whitney devised a simple machine that used a hand crank and sharp-edged teeth to separate the seeds from the cotton — the "**cotton gin**" ("gin" was short for "engine") — which revolutionized cotton production in the south. He showed it to a number of plantation owners, who were ecstatic to find that one person using the hand crank could separate as much cotton as 50 slaves working by hand. Whitney patented his invention in 1794.

Ironically, the device increased the demand for slaves. Since more cotton could be separated, more could be grown, and more field hands were needed for harvesting.

Whitney returned north, and in 1798, won a government contract to produce 10,000 muskets. He opened his Mill Rock factory in present-day Whitneyville, Connecticut.

Frustrated time and again with the process of manufacturing, he eventually turned to the idea of interchangeable parts and mass production. Prior to 1800, most of the weaponry and fine craft work in the United States had been done by hand. A customer who purchased a musket would need to return to the maker in order to have a part repaired. Whitney revolutionized this with his system. By the time he delivered his last musket to the U.S. government in 1809, Whitney's idea of interchangeable parts had spread to several other areas in New England, effectively beginning the **Industrial Revolution** in the United States.

Whitney married Henrietta Edwards in 1817. They had three children.

Whitney continued to work, and may have invented the first milling machine in 1818. Although there is some question as to whether he was truly an inventor or merely an adapter of techniques, there is no doubt that he was one of the most important and influential leaders of American industry.

16. John Quincy Adams
(1767–1848)

The son of the second president, and himself the sixth president, **John Quincy Adams** perpetuated and defined the importance of the Adams family in American political life. He was born in Braintree, Massachusetts the oldest child of **John** and **Abigail Adams** (see no. 4). He went to Europe with his father at the age of 10 and received an outstanding education in letters, languages and diplomacy. He returned to the United States and graduated from Harvard College in 1787. By 1790, he had established a law practice in Boston.

Adams's remarkable diplomatic career began when President **George Washington** (see no. 2) appointed him as minister to the Netherlands (1794–1797). In 1797, Adams's father, as president, named him minister to Prussia (1797–1801).

Returning home, Adams served as a Federalist in the U.S. Senate (1803–1808) and as a professor of oratory and rhetoric at Harvard (1806–1809). He went overseas again in 1809, as U.S. minister to Russia, where he served until 1811. Adams was one of the American negotiators at the **Treaty of Ghent** (1814), which ended the war with England. He then became minister to Great Britain (1815–1817).

While Secretary of State (1817–1825) under President **James Monroe**, he negotiated the **Adams-Onis Treaty** (1819), which obtained Florida from Spain and drew a line between American and Spanish possessions in North America all the way to the Pacific Ocean. This was the first time the country had obtained a diplomatic recognition of its own idea of manifest destiny, the quest for expansion of the United States.

In the presidential race of 1824, Adams came in second in the popular vote to **Andrew Jackson** (see no. 17), but he won the electoral election held in the U.S. House of Representatives. As president (1825–1829), Adams encountered many obstacles that did not yield to his pen, his powers of persuasion or his logic. After losing the election of 1828 to Jackson, Adams retired happily to Massachusetts.

In November 1830, the people of the Plymouth, Massachusetts congressional district voted to send him to the U.S. House of Representatives. As the only ex-president ever to sit in Congress (1831–1848), Adams cut a grand figure as "Old Man Eloquent." With nothing to lose in terms of a political future, he spoke out boldly on matters such as the abolition of slavery, the annexation of Texas, and the war with Mexico. Adams also went out of his way to represent escaped African slaves before the Supreme Court in the *Amistad* affair. He collapsed in the House and died there on February 23, 1848.

John Quincy Adams

17. Andrew Jackson
(1767–1845)

Andrew Jackson

The first "common man" to win the White House, **Andrew Jackson** was born in 1767 at Waxhaw, on the border between North and South Carolina (both states have claimed him as a native son). Born into modest circumstances and orphaned at age 14, Jackson went on to become a land speculator and was the first congressman elected in Tennessee (his home state by adoption). He then became a Tennessee senator (1797–1798), and later, a superior court judge in that state (1798–1804).

Jackson's chance to win fame arrived when he was commissioned major general of the Tennessee militia during the **War of 1812**. He fought deadly campaigns against the **Creek Indians** and won the important **Battle of Horseshoe Bend** in 1814. Given the rank of major general in the United States Army, he captured the British post of Pensacola, Florida and then ably defended New Orleans from an attack by British troops. As the hero of the **Battle of New Orleans**, Jackson gained national acclaim and prepared to advance his political ambitions.

Following an invasion of Spanish Florida in 1818 (which led to Florida's accession into the U.S.), Jackson began preparing to run for the presidency. The opening of voting rights to adult males who owned property paved the way for the election of 1824. Jackson won a plurality of the popular vote but lost the run-off election in the House of Representatives to **John Quincy Adams** (see no. 16). Furious at having been "cheated," he immediately began plans for the election of 1828, which he won easily. Inaugurated in March 1829, Jackson was the first American president to come from a state other than Massachusetts or Virginia, and the first who was not a man of great wealth.

Jackson's two-term presidency (1829–1837) saw major developments he considered to be triumphs, but this view has been questioned by historians. He ejected the **Five Civilized Tribes** (Choctaw, Chickasaw, Cherokee, Seminole and Creek) from the American southeast (to across the Mississippi River) and forced the state of South Carolina to abandon its ideas of secession. He "killed" the **Bank of the United States**, which he believed was the root of the economic problems of American farmers.

Jackson was an aggressive president, using his veto privilege far more than his predecessors, and quickly removing from office those government officials who opposed him. Nevertheless, he left office in a blaze of popularity and glory that was not eclipsed even by the **Panic of 1837**, which his anti-bank attitude had helped create.

He retired to Hermitage, his home near Nashville, Tennessee and remained the elder statesman of American politics until his death. Jackson personified the ruthlessness and intensity of the American frontiersman during the first half of the 19th century. He redefined the American presidency, making it a much more powerful institution than the one he had entered in 1829.

18. Tecumseh
(c. 1768–1813)

Born near the Mad River in what is now Greene County, Ohio, the future **Shawnee Indian** chief **Tecumseh** grew up in a time of dwindling opportunity for his tribe. The Shawnees had been ejected from western Virginia by white settlers and were forced to resettle north of the Ohio River. In Tecumseh they found a champion who would fight for their cause, and indeed for the cause of all Native Americans who were willing to resist the encroachments of the white men on their territory.

Tecumseh fought as an ally of the British during the **American Revolution**. In the early 1790s, he served as a scout for Miami chief **Little Turtle**, and his efforts led to the remarkable Indian victory over the Americans. After the Americans defeated the tribal forces at the **Battle of Fallen Timbers** (1794), Tecumseh refused to attend the peace treaty at Greenville, Ohio in 1795.

It may have been at this time he formulated what became the central point of his beliefs: that the land of North America belonged to all the tribes collectively, and no tribe could therefore legally cede land to the whites.

In the late 1790s, Tecumseh fell in love with Rebecca Galloway, the daughter of a white settler in Ohio. She taught him to read and opened his mind to the accomplishments of past military leaders such as Caesar and Charlemagne. Tecumseh asked her to marry him, but her condition that he abandon his Native American ways proved too much for

Tecumseh

him to bear, and the marriage did not take place.

By 1808, Tecumseh and his younger brother **Tenskwatawa** (meaning "the Open Door") had established a religious community they called **Prophet's Town** on the bank of the Wabash River in Indiana, near its confluence with the Tippecanoe River. In July 1811, Tecumseh attempted, with limited success, to persuade Native Americans in the Carolinas, Georgia, Florida, Arkansas and Alabama to join him in a true tribal confederacy. Upon his return to Prophet's Town, he found that General **William Henry Harrison**, governor of the Indiana Territory, had moved in 1,100 troops. A battle had been fought at the mouth of the Tippecanoe, and the Americans prevailed. Furious with his brother for having entered into conflict in his absence, Tecumseh sent Tenskwatawa west.

The start of the **War of 1812** brought hope to Tecumseh and his followers a new ally, the British in Canada. He and British general Isaac Brock worked together and captured Fort Detroit from the Americans. Brock was killed that same year, and his successor, Colonel Henry Proctor, was both timid and contemptuous of his Native American allies. Following a series of American victories, Tecumseh persuaded Proctor to make a stand at the Battle of the Thames River in present-day Ontario. Tecumseh was killed while exhorting his men to keep fighting.

This renowned pair of American explorers both came from Virginia. **Meriwether Lewis** was born in Albemarle County and **William Clark** in Caroline County. Lewis joined the American Army in 1795, and in his first campaign, he was a subordinate of Clark's, who was captain of the Chosen Rifle Company of sharpshooters. While the two men served together, Clark made an impression on Lewis that the younger man did not forget.

Summoned by President **Thomas Jefferson** (see no. 8) to serve as his private secretary, Lewis spent the years 1801–1803 in Washington, D.C. Jefferson named him as leader of the exploratory expedition he wanted to send across the continent in order to facilitate trade and relations with the Native Americans. There was soon the added incentive of exploring the land that came to the United States under the terms of the **Louisiana Purchase**. Lewis wrote to Clark, asking him to serve as joint commander of the expedition. Clark agreed, and the two men recruited a small group of hardy explorers.

On May 21, 1804, Lewis, Clark and approximately 47 men left St. Charles (in present-day Missouri), near St. Louis. They spent that year ascending the Missouri River and reached

William Clark

the villages of the **Mandan Indians** in present-day North Dakota. They were fortunate to win the friendship of an Indian woman, **Sacajawea**, who went on to assist them as a guide and interpreter.

The explorers crossed the **Continental Divide** and began their descent toward the west coast. They reached the headwaters of the Columbia River and built canoes in which they paddled steadily westward. The company spent the winter at **Fort Clatsop** on the southern bank of the river, near present-day Astoria, Oregon, and began its return journey in the spring of 1806.

On September 23, 1806, Lewis, Clark, and all but one of their men returned to St. Louis where they were greeted with great joy; they had been given up for dead some time before. Their remarkable journey had defined the northern corridor of what would become the U.S.-Canadian border and disproved the notion that an all-water route could be found across the mountains.

Lewis served as territorial governor of Louisiana (1807–1809) and died under mysterious circumstances in 1809. Clark served as both brigadier general of the Louisiana Territory and superintendent for Indian Affairs at St. Louis.

Meriwether Lewis

One of the longest and most distinguished careers in American politics belonged to **Henry Clay** of Kentucky, but the silver-tongued orator never managed to achieve the summit of his ambitions — to be president of the United States. Born in Hanover County, Virginia in 1777, Clay was admitted to the Virginia bar in 1797. That same year, he left for Lexington, Kentucky.

Clay served as defense counsel for **Aaron Burr** in 1806, and was named to fill an unexpired term in the U.S. Senate that year at the age of 28. After one year, Clay returned to his home state where he served in the legislature between 1807 and 1810. In 1810, he went to Washington, D.C. again to fill another unexpired senatorial term. Finally, he was elected to the U.S. House of Representatives in 1811.

Clay became the first true Speaker of the House of Representatives and served in that capacity six times. He was a formidable "**War Hawk**" during the **War of 1812**. After the war was over, he developed and presented his idea for an "American System" of manufacturing, transportation and public improvements he said would make the United States the envy of the world. Often passionate in his oratory, and generally persuasive, Clay managed to bring the northern and southern states to the **Missouri Compromise** of 1820, under which Maine entered the Union as a free state and Missouri as a slave state. His work in this matter gained him the title of "**The Great Pacificator**."

Clay ran for president in 1824. Failing to win the election, he nevertheless was appointed Secretary of State by the new president, **John Quincy Adams** (see no. 16), a post Clay held for the next four years. He re-entered the U.S. Senate in 1831 and became the obvious challenger to President **Andrew Jackson** (see no. 17) in the presidential election of 1832. Clay won only 49 electoral votes to Jackson's 219. Even the Great Pacificator could not overcome the reputation and popularity of "Old Hickory." Clay remained in the Senate until 1842.

Upon his resignation from the Senate, he prepared for another run for the presidency. As the Whig party candidate in 1844, he lost to Democrat **James K. Polk** by a margin of 65 electoral votes.

Discouraged by his repeated setbacks, Clay retired to his estate in Louisville, Kentucky. He returned to the Senate in 1849 to render one last great service to the country. Through his negotiations with southern and northern legislators he paved the way for the **Compromise of 1850**, which prevented an outright break between the north and south that year. He answered the first roll call in the Senate in 1852, then succumbed to tuberculosis, dying at the National Hotel in Washington, D.C.

Henry Clay

Roger Taney
(1777–1864)

Roger Taney

The fifth Chief Justice of the United States, **Roger B. Taney** was born in Calvert County, Maryland on an estate that had been in the Taney family for generations. He graduated from Dickinson College in 1795 and was admitted to the bar in 1799.

He served in the Maryland House of Delegates for one year (1800) before setting up a private law practice in Frederick, Maryland. Taney served again in the state legislature (1816–1821) and rose to the position of attorney general of Maryland in 1827. In 1831, he was named Attorney General of the United States.

Eager to eliminate the **Bank of the United States** (chartered in 1811), President **Andrew Jackson** (see no. 17) named Taney as Secretary of the Treasury in 1833. Taney followed Jackson's desires and withdrew funds from the national bank, allocating them to state or "pet" banks, as they were called by opponents of the idea. In June 1834, the U.S. Senate rejected Taney's nomination as treasury secretary. In 1835, the same Senate rejected his nomination for associate justice of the Supreme Court. Therefore, it came as a great surprise when Jackson nominated Taney for Chief Justice of the United States upon the death of **John Marshall** (see no. 11) — and an even greater surprise when the Senate confirmed the nomination!

Generally, Taney favored the interests of the federal government over those of the individual states. Taney's rulings in *Charles River Bridge Co. v. Warren Bridge Co.* (1837), *Cooley v. Board of Port Wardens* (1852) and *The Genesee Chief v. Fitzhugh* (1852) all added further definitions to federal and state rights that had not been previously elucidated.

Taney's most important decision came in the famous **Dred Scott** case, officially known as *Scott v. Sanford* (1857). Although he was personally opposed to slavery, and had in fact freed all the slaves he had inherited, Taney found that a strict interpretation of the **Constitution** required him to submit the following decision: (1), that Congress had no right to ban slavery from the different territories, and (2), that African-Americans were ineligible for U.S. citizenship.

He issued one very important, and often-overlooked, ruling in *Ex Parte Merryman* (1861), declaring that President **Abraham Lincoln** (see no. 34) could not suspend *habeas corpus*, even in time of civil war. Unfortunately, this move came too late to rescue Taney's reputation, and he went down in history as the judge who issued the Dred Scott decision, thereby appearing to favor the interests of southern slaveholders.

22. Daniel Webster
(1782–1852)

The "God-like Dan'l" occupied center stage in American oratory and politics for two generations and remains one of the icons of American political leadership. Born in Salisbury, New Hampshire in 1782, **Daniel Webster** graduated from Dartmouth College in 1801 and proceeded to study law. Admitted to the bar in 1805, he began to practice in Boscawen, New Hampshire and then moved to Portsmouth in 1807.

Webster represented, first, New Hampshire (1813–1817), and then, Massachusetts (1823–1827) in the U.S. House of Representatives. He laid the basis for his popularity and reputation while acting as counsel for the trustees of Dartmouth College in the famous *Dartmouth College v. Woodward* Supreme Court case of 1818. His success on that occasion made him the most in-demand speaker in America. He went on to deliver key addresses at the Plymouth Rock bicentennial (1820) and the laying of the cornerstone of the Bunker Hill monument (1825).

Chosen to succeed a deceased member of the U.S. Senate in 1827, Webster became even more renowned when he delivered to the Senate his famous **"Reply to Hayne"** in January 1830. Arguing against the southern idea of **nullification**, Webster delivered a passionate and thrilling speech (which ran to 73 printed pages of text!) that concluded with the words "Liberty and Union, now and forever, one and inseparable!" There was no doubt that Webster carried the day. This speech enshrined the cause for which hundreds of thousands of Americans would give their lives during the **Civil War** (1861-1865).

Webster ran as a Whig candidate for president in 1836, but received few votes. He served as U.S. Secretary of State (1841–1843 and 1850–1852), and negotiated the **Webster-Ashburton Treaty**, which drew the present-day boundary between Maine and Canada.

On March 7, 1850, he delivered a calm speech in the Senate, urging the nation's leaders to follow his lead in compromising over slavery. "I wish to speak today not as a Massachusetts man, nor as a northern man, but as an American. I speak today for the preservation of the Union. Hear me for my cause." Although he was denounced by

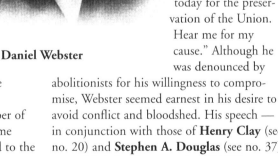

Daniel Webster

abolitionists for his willingness to compromise, Webster seemed earnest in his desire to avoid conflict and bloodshed. His speech — in conjunction with those of **Henry Clay** (see no. 20) and **Stephen A. Douglas** (see no. 37) — enabled the **Compromise of 1850** to come into form, thereby delaying the agonies of civil war for 10 years. Webster died at his home in Marshfield, Massachusetts.

John C. Calhoun
(1782–1850)

One of the handful of leaders who dominated American politics between 1812 and the **Civil War** was **John C. Calhoun**, born near Calhoun Mills in Abbeville County, South Carolina. He went north and graduated from Yale College in 1804. Returning home, he was admitted to the bar in 1807 and opened an office in Abbeville.

Calhoun was elected to the South Carolina legislature in 1808. In 1810, he was elected as a Democratic-Republican to the U.S. House of Representatives where he served until 1817. Referred to as the "Young Hercules," he carried many of the burdens of the **War of 1812**. He participated in every significant congressional decision during the war and was committed to seeing the matter through to completion. This service led to the post of Secretary of War, which he held from 1817 until 1825. He won the vice presidency, serving under President **John Quincy Adams** (see no. 16) from 1825 to 1829.

Calhoun won the vice presidency a second time in the election of 1828 and served under **Andrew Jackson** (see no. 17). Up to this point, Calhoun had been a confirmed nationalist, but the **Tariff of 1828** infuriated many southerners, and he voiced their anger in his *South Carolina Exposition* (1828). Calhoun enunciated the doctrine of "**nullification**," meaning that a state should have the power to

John C. Calhoun

nullify a federal law within the borders of that state if the federal law worked directly against the interests of that state.

Calhoun's stand on southern sectionalism and states' rights led him into conflict with Jackson. The president and vice president tangled with each other repeatedly, and in 1832, Calhoun resigned so he could take a Senate seat. In the same year, South Carolina did seek to nullify the Tariff of 1828, but it rescinded the nullification under the threat of invasion by federal troops. Calhoun, who believed in states' rights but not in revolution, found himself the spokesperson for the south from that point on.

Calhoun served in the Senate (1832–1844), then as Secretary of State (1844–1845) in the final year of **John Tyler**'s presidency, and returned to the Senate in 1846, where he remained until his death. He engineered the passing of "gag rules" that prohibited the discussion of slavery in Congress and became more definitely sectional in his opinions.

To ill to speak, on March 4, 1850, his last speech was read to the Senate. Regarding the political crisis of 1850, over whether to admit California to the Union, Calhoun insisted that if the north attempted to abolish slavery, then the southern states would be forced to consider leaving the Union — an action he believed was permissible under the Constitution. Calhoun died on March 31, 1850.

Davy Crockett
(1786–1836)

Perhaps the most famous of all American frontiersmen, **David Crockett** was born near present-day Rogersville, in eastern Tennessee. One of nine children, he grew up working on his father's farm and herded cattle as far as Virginia.

Crockett tried his hand at farming, but he was much better suited to hunting. He served as a scout for Andrew Jackson's army during the **Creek War** (1813–1814), but left the service before the war was over. During the war, Crockett coined his most famous phrase, "I leave this rule for others when I'm dead, Be always sure you're right — then go ahead," recorded to history in *Narrative of the Life of Colonel Crockett* (1834).

Crockett moved to the Obion River area in southwestern Tennessee where the nearest neighbor was seven miles away. He was elected to the state legislature in 1821, where he supported bills that favored squatters and the less fortunate. He moved again, in 1823, to the western edge of Tennessee. Crockett spent eight to nine months hunting exclusively for bear; he claimed to have killed 105 during that period. Either impressed with his hunting skills, or perhaps because they simply liked Crockett, his new neighbors sent him again to the state legislature. Feeling his political oats, Crockett ran for the U.S. House of Representatives in 1825 and lost.

He ran again in 1827, and served first as a Democrat (1827–1831), then as a Whig (1833–1835) in the House of Representatives. In the spring of 1834 he conducted a well-recorded "tour of the north," where people of cities such as Boston, New York, Philadelphia and Baltimore saw the famous bear-hunting congressman in person. Despite his overall popularity, Crockett was defeated for re-election in 1835.

Crockett left Tennessee in early 1836 and headed for the growing territory of Texas, which

Davy Crockett

was claimed both by the Mexican government and the Americans who had settled there during the previous 15 years. In February, he arrived at the **Alamo** in San Antonio and offered his services to the Texas rebels under Colonel **William B. Travis** (1809–1836). Little is known of the manner in which Crockett died, but like the other 183 defenders of the Alamo, he gave his life in defense of the fort. The Mexican victory was followed in April by a Texan victory at **San Jacinto** that won independence for Texas, which became a U.S. state in 1845.

Crockett was amused by most aspects of politics and seldom concealed his disdain for city dwellers. In spite of this, he gained a large popular following during his lifetime and left a legacy of the rugged bear-hunter that has remained a part of American folklore to this day.

Samuel Morse

Telegraph inventor **Samuel F. B. Morse** was born in Charlestown, Massachusetts. Morse attended Phillips Academy in Andover, Massachusetts and graduated from Yale College in 1810.

He worked as a clerk in Charlestown for a time, then took a ship to London (1811) with the painter **Washington Allston** (1779–1843), with whom he studied art. Returning to the United States after the **War of 1812** had ended (1815), Morse set up an artist studio in Boston. Determined to revive public interest in 15th century art, he found, instead, that the only way to support himself was as a portrait painter.

Morse spent the winters of 1818–1821 in Charleston, South Carolina. In 1823, he moved permanently to New York City to find inclusion in the art society of that city. His most significant artistic success was a set of portraits he painted of the aged **Marquis de Lafayette** on the Frenchman's tour of the United States in 1825. Morse was one of the founders of the National Academy of Design and served as the first president of that organization (1826–1842). Morse spent three years in France and Italy (1829–1832), seeking again to expand his artistic senses.

The single greatest change in his life and career occurred on board the ship *Sully* during his return from Europe in 1832. Morse kept detailed notebooks that show that he first conceived of a telegraph message device during the voyage home.

Between 1832 and 1837, Morse slowly shifted from artist to inventor. With the assistance of **Leonard Dunnell Gale**, and the financial backing of **Alfred Vail**, he designed a sending and receiving apparatus that used dots and spaces to convey numbers and letters. The "**Morse Code**" was patented in 1837, then Morse spent seven long, lean years trying to persuade the governments of England and France to sponsor its use.

Failing in this, he finally found success on March 3, 1843, when in the closing moments of its final meeting, Congress voted $30,000 for the support of the telegraph. After industrialist **Ezra Cornell** (1800–1874) erected a set of wires between Washington, D.C. and Baltimore, Maryland, Morse sent his famous first message, "What hath God wrought?," from the Supreme Court in the Capital to Alfred Vail in Baltimore, 40 miles away.

Although he spent a number of frustrating years in litigation against both opponents and detractors of his invention, Morse became a wealthy man later in life. He received numerous medals from European governments, and his fame grew around the world. He was one of the founders of **Vassar College** in 1861.

26. Sam Houston
(1793–1863)

One of the most charismatic Americans of the 19th century, **Sam Houston** embodied both the American belief in helping the underdog and the American vision of "manifest destiny." Born at Timber Ridge Church in Rockbridge County, Virginia, Houston and his siblings moved with their mother to Tennessee in 1807, after the death of their father. Houston lived with the Cherokee Indians for three years, who called him "the Raven."

He joined the U.S. Army in 1813 and rose to the rank of lieutenant while serving under **Andrew Jackson** (see no. 17) in the **Creek War** (1813–1814). He resigned from the army to practice law in Lebanon, Tennessee. Within one year of passing the bar, he became the state's attorney general. This position led to his election to the U.S. House of Representatives as a Democrat (1823–1827). Houston then ran for and won the office of state governor, but his term in office (1827–1829) was cut short by an unfortunate marriage to Eliza Allen in 1829. The couple separated after only three months. Houston resigned the governorship and left Tennessee for the Arkansas Territory to live with members of the Cherokee tribe west of the Mississippi River.

Settling in present-day Oklahoma, Houston became a member of the Cherokee nation and entered a common-law marriage with Tiana Rogers, a Cherokee woman. Resenting the treatment of his fellow Native Americans by white settlers, Houston went to Washington, D.C. in 1832. There he assaulted a member of Congress after a bitter dispute with the man over Native-American

Sam Houston

rights. He received a formal congressional reprimand for the action.

Later the same year, Houston left the Cherokees to go to Texas. Sensing the people were about to revolt against Mexican rule, he supported a strong stand for Texan independence. Early in 1836, he was named commander-in-chief of the Texas army. Following losses at the **Alamo** and **Goliad**, Houston led 800 Texans in a complete victory over Mexican leader **Santa Anna** (1797–1876) at the **Battle of San Jacinto** (April 21, 1836).

Houston became the first president of the **Republic of Texas** (1836–1838), served in the Texas legislature (1838–1840), and served as president again (1841–1844). He married for the third time to Margaret Lea of Alabama (1840); the couple had eight children.

After Texas became one of the United States (1845), Houston served as a Democratic senator in Washington, D.C. (1846–1859). During the tumultuous years leading up to the **Civil War**, he was one of the few southern political leaders who were vehemently opposed to the idea of secession from the Union.

Houston was elected governor of Texas in 1859; he was deposed from office on March 18, 1861, after refusing to take an oath of loyalty to the **Confederate States of America**. He retired to his ranch and lived long enough to witness the proof of his belief that secession would be disastrous for the state and the country as a whole. Legislator, governor, congressman, senator and friend of the Native Americans, Sam Houston defied many stereotypes of the 19th century.

27. Cornelius Vanderbilt
(1794–1877)

Born at Port Richmond on Staten Island, New York, **Cornelius Vanderbilt** began life with no obvious advantages. He ended his schooling at the age of 11 and began to assist his father in small boating operations around New York Harbor. In 1810, he bought a ferryboat and began his own passenger and freight (farm products) service between Staten Island and New York City. The start of the War of 1812 assisted the growth of his business; Vanderbilt won government contracts for supplying the forts that guarded the harbor to America's most valuable port city.

In 1813, he married his first cousin, Sophia Johnson, with whom he eventually had a total of 13 children.

Between 1815 and 1818 Vanderbilt came to own a number of commercial vessels that plied the waters between New England and the Carolinas. In 1818, he surprised everyone by selling all his ships and going to work as a captain for Thomas Gibbons' steamboat line between New Brunswick, New Jersey and New York City. Vanderbilt made excellent use of his time under Gibbons (1818–1829), learned the steamboat business, and was prepared to launch his own steamship line on the Hudson River in 1829. Meanwhile, Gibbons made transportation history by winning the Supreme Court case *Gibbons v. Ogden* (1824), which outlawed a commercial monopoly that had been granted to **Robert Fulton** (see no. 14) a number of years earlier.

The man now known as "Commodore" Vanderbilt went from one success to another. By the 1840s, his steamboats traveled the Hudson River, Long Island Sound and the New England coast. In 1850, he financed and established a combined steamship and roadway passage that brought passengers across the Central American isthmus at **Nicaragua** instead of the traditional crossing at **Panama**. Vanderbilt's ingenuity cut two days off the travel time between New York and San Francisco, allowing him to reduce costs and drive out his competitors.

Vanderbilt and his large family took the first vacation of his lifetime in 1853, making a triumphal tour of Europe. He sold his steamboat interests in 1858 and, as he neared the age of 70, changed his business interest to railroads.

In 1862 and 1863 he bought a controlling interest in the **New York and Harlem Railroad;** he expanded to buy up the **Hudson River Railroad**, and by 1867, he controlled the **New York Central Railway** line between Albany and Buffalo. He acquired the **Lake Shore and Michigan Southern Railroad** in 1873, and then picked up the **Canada Southern Railway** (1874), which extended the domain of his operations all the way to Chicago. Vanderbilt then had **Grand Central** terminal built in New York City.

Vanderbilt died in New York City in 1877, leaving an estate worth more than $100 million. He made a bequest of nearly one million dollars to the Central University of Nashville, which later was renamed **Vanderbilt University** in his honor. He left $90 million to his son William, and $7.5 million to William's four sons. A confirmed male chauvinist, he distributed a paltry $4 million among his eight daughters. "Commodore" Vanderbilt had built a transportation empire with few rivals during the middle of the 19th century.

Cornelius Vanderbilt

28. James K. Polk
(1795–1849)

The 11th president of the United States, **James K. Polk** was born on the family farm in Mecklenburg County, North Carolina. The oldest of 10 children, he was sickly as a youth.

Polk graduated at the head of his class from the University of North Carolina in 1818. He read in Tennessee law under **Felix Grundy** (1777–1840) in Nashville. When the Panic of 1819 threatened his future, Grundy had him named as clerk of the Tennessee Senate. Polk was admitted to the bar in 1820 and elected to the lower house of the Tennessee legislature for the first time in 1823.

On January 1, 1824, he married Sarah Childress. The couple had no children, but they formed a remarkably solid and equal partnership that endured throughout their years together.

In the legislature, Polk started on the side of the opposition to land speculators and bankers (perhaps from his memory of the 1819 panic). He then changed to support the fortunes of the rising star of Tennessee — **Andrew Jackson** (see no. 17), the head of the land speculators — and indeed, the entire south.

Elected to the U.S. House of Representatives in 1824, Polk became one of Jackson's most loyal supporters in Washington, D.C. Even after Jackson and another prominent southerner, **John C. Calhoun** (see no. 23), parted ways, Polk remained true to Jackson, thereby earning himself the role of Speaker of the House of Representatives (1835–1839).

Polk returned to Tennessee to serve as governor (1839–1841), but was defeated in his two attempts (1841, 1843) to win a second term. In 1844, he was considered a likely candidate for the Democratic vice presidential nomination, but a surprising turn of events brought him forward as the first "dark horse" candidate in American political history.

James K. Polk

However, he beat **Henry Clay** (see no. 20) in the national election to win the White House.

Polk's one-term presidency (1845–1849) was effective and to the point. Upon entering the White House, he said he had four goals: to lower the tariff, stop spending on internal improvements, settle the Oregon boundary dispute with Great Britain, and win California for the United States. He succeeded on nearly every count. The **Mexican War** brought California and all of the present-day American southwest under the "Stars and Stripes." Spending was reduced, as was the tariff. Polk's only semi-failure was that he could not achieve his election slogan of "Fifty-four forty or fight," which referred to the 54th parallel of latitude. Instead, the United States compromised with England and drew the boundary between Canada and the Oregon Territory (present-day Washington) at the 49th parallel of north latitude.

Still in poor health, Polk was worn out by his successes. He feuded with his two most prominent generals, **Winfield Scott** and **Zachary Taylor**, and did so much paperwork that he did not have the energy to run for a second term. He retired to his homestead and died in Nashville just three months after leaving office.

John Brown
(1800–1859)

John Brown

"John Brown's body lies a-mouldering in the grave, but his soul is marching on." These words were sung by hundreds of thousands of Union soldiers during the **Civil War**, in tribute to the moral legacy left by one remarkable individual. Born in Torrington, Connecticut, **John Brown** experienced considerable dislocation throughout his life. His family moved to Hudson, Ohio in 1804, where he grew up working with his father as a farmer and tanner.

Brown worked as a farmer in Randolph, Pennsylvania and raised sheep wool in Ohio before the second part of his business went bankrupt in 1835. By the late 1840s, he became a vigorous abolitionist, believing that the Bible and simple morality clearly dictated the necessity of freeing the African-Americans held in slavery. Brown's home in Pennsylvania had a concealed room to hide runaway slaves.

In 1849, he moved to North Elba, New York, a free black community near Lake Placid and the American-Canadian border.

Always a man of action, he became incensed when news spread of the **Kansas-Nebraska Act** (1854), which allowed the people of the Kansas and Nebraska territories to decide whether they would allow slavery within their borders. On May 24, 1856, along with four of his sons and two other men, he carried out an attack against five pro-slavery men at Osawatomie, Kansas, in retaliation for a pro-slavery raid that had occurred three days earlier. From that time on, Brown's fame and infamy spread. He became known as "Captain" John Brown and "Osawatomie Brown."

Brown led an abolitionist raid into the slave state of Missouri in 1858 and brought many African-Americans on the 1,000-mile trek to freedom in Canada. He then went eastward and planned an ambitious attempt to provide Virginia slaves with weapons and ammunition. Brown, 13 whites, and five African-Americans seized the federal arsenal at **Harper's Ferry**, Virginia (now West Virginia) on October 16, 1859. His effort did not bring the hundreds or thousands of slaves he had hoped for, and on October 17, federal troops under the command of **Robert E. Lee** (1807–1870) surrounded the complex, fought a short battle, and captured Brown.

Tried in Charles Town, Virginia (present-day West Virginia), between October 27 and October 31, and sentenced to death, Brown was hanged on December 2, 1859. He made no pleas for mercy, instead, he affirmed the necessity for all men of conscience to follow him in the goal of abolition. Brown's striking demeanor at the trial and prior to his execution caused many northerners to regard him as a hero. To southerners, he remained the epitome of all that they feared and distrusted.

30. Brigham Young
(1801–1877)

The single most successful American religious leader of the 19th century, **Brigham Young** was born the ninth of 11 children to John and Abigail Young in Whitingham, Vermont. The family moved to a district in upstate New York that had seen a rapid succession of evangelistic ministers.

Having shown little interest in religion during his youth, Young took his time examining the faith of the new Mormon church, led by **Joseph Smith**. In 1832, Young left the Methodist church and was baptized into the Mormon faith. He was named by Smith as one of the Twelve Apostles of the new faith. Young undertook an extensive period of evangelical ministry in England from 1839 to 1841, where he first published the Mormon newspaper, *Millennial Star*. He returned to the United States, and, following the murder of Joseph Smith at Nauvoo, Illinois in 1844, he became the new leader of the Mormon church.

Seeking an alternative to living near "gentile" (i.e., non-Mormon) communities, Young decided to relocate his flock to a place in the far west where his people would not be harassed. He directed a full-scale immigration between 1844 and 1846, leading the Mormons to the Valley of the Great Salt Lake, in what is now Utah. Young's first sighting of the valley took place July 24, 1847. He immediately approved the location, and the Mormons soon began work to create a civilization of their own, far removed from other Americans.

Brigham Young

Young and his followers experienced considerable success in farming, the use of canals and irrigation, and the promotion of further immigration. During his lifetime, 70,000 converts came from Europe to Utah. The only disappointment was that the Mormons would not enjoy the new land completely for themselves. The **Mexican War** and the California **gold rush** brought thousands of gentiles through Utah, and Young feared for the sanctity and purity of his flock. The primary cause of contention between the Mormons and gentiles was the Mormon practice of polygamy; Young himself had a total of 27 wives and 56 children.

Young was appointed governor of the Utah Territory in 1850. Subsequent encroachment of gentiles brought on by developments such as the building of the transcontinental railroad (completed in 1869) did not significantly change his plans to build and strengthen the Mormon church. He remained steadfast in his beliefs until his death, by which time the Mormon population had grown to 140,000 settlers. The Mormon church renounced polygamy in 1890 and Utah became a state in 1896.

Dorothea Dix

The concept of the "wounded healer" might well be applied to the turbulent life of **Dorothea Dix**. Born in Hampden, Maine as Dorothea Lynde, she fled her family home by the age of 12.

With the help of her grandmother, she began teaching school in Worcester, Massachusetts, in 1816. She continued in her profession, founding a "dame school" in Boston (1821), where, a student later recalled, she exercised an iron will over her students.

Worn down from exhaustion, she left teaching in 1824 and wrote a number of children's books, including *Hymns for Children* (1825) and *Meditations for Private Hours* (1828). By her mid-to-late thirties, Dix showed every evidence of falling into the anonymity and semi-poverty that most unmarried women were expected to endure in the 19th century.

Instead she found a new calling. On March 28, 1841, she went to teach a Sunday school class at the East Cambridge, Massachusetts house of correction. Horrified by the appalling conditions under which the prisoners lived and the fact that insane people were held in the same cells as murderers and thieves, she determined to bring about a change. Dix conducted an 18-month survey of every jail, almshouse and house of correction in the state. In January 1843, she brought before the Massachusetts legislature news of what she had found. After considerable debate and argument, the legislature appropriated funds to expand the state institution for the insane in Worcester. This was one of the most memorable of Dix's many victories in her crusade to promote better conditions for the insane and the incarcerated.

She took her cause to many states. Time and again she shamed state legislators into providing funds for the improvement of treatment facilities. Dix became a household name in the United States, and she used her new influence to promote her book *Remarks on Prisons and Prison Discipline in the United States* (1845).

Dix went overseas to England, France, Turkey, Russia and Italy. She met **Pope Pius IX** at the Vatican and persuaded him to do more to help the cause of the insane in Rome. Dix returned home in 1856 and served as superintendent of Union Army nurses during the **Civil War**.

She retired to the hospital she had helped design in Trenton and died there in 1887. The measure of her success can be found in one startling statistic: In 1843, there were only 13 mental hospitals in the United States. By 1880, there were 123, of which 32 had been founded directly through her efforts.

32. Ralph Waldo Emerson
(1803–1882)

"There is properly no history; only biography," wrote **Ralph Waldo Emerson** in his *Essays*. Emerson's many biographers remain mystified to some extent by the writer's life and beliefs. How can one man have had such an influence on 19th and 20th century American thought?

Born in Boston, Massachusetts, Emerson was the third of six sons of a Unitarian minister, who died when Emerson was seven years old. Through heroic efforts, Emerson's mother ensured that her four surviving sons all attended Boston Latin School and graduated from Harvard College. Emerson graduated in 1821. He then proceeded to teach school, which he found vaguely dissatisfying.

Emerson went to Europe (1832–1835) and traveled throughout England, France and Italy. He came back full of the images and words of the Romantic artists and writers of that period. He gave public lectures in Massachusetts on subjects such as "The Uses of Natural History" and "The American Scholar" (the latter was his address to the Harvard graduating class of 1837). Emerson moved to Concord, Massachusetts in 1834 where his home became a haven for writers and conversationalists who soon formed the core of what would be labeled the **Transcendentalist** movement.

Emerson helped launch the literary magazine *Dial* in 1840 and served for two years as its editor. He went abroad again in 1847, renewing his acquaintances with many of the prominent writers and poets in England.

He returned to the United States and soon faced, as did all his fellows, the traumas of disharmony that would lead to the **Civil War**. Never an ardent activist, he did support the abolition movement, and came out firmly for the North during the Civil War.

Emerson's finest works had been accomplished before 1860. After that time, his writ-

Ralph Waldo Emerson

ing became more repetitious than inspiring. He died of pneumonia in Concord in 1882.

Emerson strove to bring about a new understanding of the ancient concepts of nature and spirit, reason and understanding. Believing that a human being's true genius lay in individuality, Emerson stressed intellectual and moral self-reliance and encouraged all people to act and think for themselves. What he intended was to refine American thought, to grace it with subtle understanding and wisdom.

Some 20th century scholars have asserted that Emerson's stress on individualism has actually led to more brutish forms of behavior and attitude, such as the later examples of the selfish "ugly American." If there is any truth to this claim, Emerson would have been shocked to find that his ideas had been construed to give legitimacy to a self-centered and macho ethic.

The distinction of being the first and only Confederate president went to a Mississippi plantation owner who believed slavery was a positive good that needed to be preserved. Born in Christian County (present-day Todd County), Kentucky, **Jefferson Davis** was the youngest of 10 children. The Davis family soon moved to the cotton-growing region of Wilkinson County, Mississippi, where he grew up.

Davis attended Transylvania College but graduated from the U.S. Military Academy at West Point in 1828. Serving with the U.S. Army in the Pacific northwest, he met Sarah Knox, the daughter of his commanding officer, **Zachary Taylor** (1784–1850). Davis resigned from the army in 1835 and married Knox; the couple went to live on a 1,000-acre cotton plantation given to them by Davis' older brother Joseph.

Jefferson Davis

Davis entered the Mississippi legislature in 1843. He served in the U.S. House of Representatives briefly before serving as commander of the Mississippi Rifles in the **Mexican War**. Under the watchful eye of Taylor, Davis fought with distinction at **Monterey** and the **Battle of Buena Vista**, where he was wounded. Returning home a hero, he served in the U.S. Senate (1847–1851) and as U.S. Secretary of War (1853–1857). Elected to the Senate again in 1857, he became the recognized advocate for the southern way of life: plantations, cotton and slavery.

Although he was only a moderate secessionist, Davis was selected by the **Provisional Congress of the Confederacy** in 1861 to be president of the **Confederate States of America**. Davis appointed men of high ability to his cabinet and was totally committed to governing the South during the war years. However, he lacked the important skills of humor, tact and conciliation that his opponent, **Abraham Lincoln** (see no. 34), possessed to such a high degree.

By early 1865, Davis had lost the confidence of the southern people, and fled from the Confederate capital of Richmond, Virginia on April 3, 1865. He was taken prisoner at Irwinville, Georgia and held for two years at Fortress Monroe in Virginia. Although he was indicted twice, he never was called to trial and was released on May 13, 1867. The fact that he had briefly been held with leg shackles had won the sympathy of many southerners, and he regained his stature among them by the time of his release.

Davis never asked for, or received, a pardon for his role in the **Civil War**. He retired to Mississippi and wrote *The Rise and Fall of the Confederate Government* (1881), in which he defended the decisions that had been made in 1861. He died in New Orleans, Louisiana in 1889.

34. Abraham Lincoln
(1809–1865)

Perhaps the most loved and admired American since the time of his death, **Abraham Lincoln** has become the most consistent icon of American political biography: the man from a log cabin who rose in life and changed the world he knew, consistently remaining humble and forgiving.

The second child of Thomas Lincoln and the former Nancy Hanks, Lincoln was born near Hodgenville, Kentucky. The family moved to Indiana in 1816 and to Illinois in 1830.

He was elected to the Illinois House of Representatives, where he served from 1835 to 1841, and earned his law license in 1836. Lincoln served in the U.S. House of Representatives (1847–1849), where he opposed the **Mexican War**.

Returning to Illinois, he found his political interests fading until the controversy of the **Kansas-Nebraska Act** (1854) brought him back to the fore. He lost a race for the U.S. Senate in 1854 and changed his political affiliation to the new Republican party in 1856. He then engaged in the famous **Lincoln-Douglas Debates** (August 21–October 15, 1858) and emerged as a spokesman for many northerners, although he was at most a lukewarm abolitionist at the time. His speech at New York's Cooper Union in 1860 won him many admirers, and in November, he won the presidential election by a plurality.

As president, Lincoln charted dangerous waters in many respects. Seeking at first to win the war to save the Union, he found that events prompted him to slowly move into the ranks of the true abolitionists. In September 1862, he issued the **Emancipation Proclamation**, freeing the slaves in all states still in rebellion, effective January 1, 1863. Having now doubled the reasons for fighting, he sought to find a general capable of winning the war. Generals **Ulysses S. Grant** (see no. 45) and **William T. Sherman** brought that victory to the Union armies in 1864–1865.

Another major challenge for Lincoln was to walk a fine line between those who wanted to punish the South severely (the Radical Republicans) and those who advocated a more lenient course. He succeeded in many respects. His **Gettysburg Address** (1863) was a triumph of oration, and eloquently described the meaning of the war. Lincoln won reelection in 1864, and in his second inaugural address stated that mercy should dictate the peace that followed.

Abraham Lincoln

With the surrender of General **Robert E. Lee**'s army on April 9, 1865, Lincoln thought his work was nearly complete.

In a rare moment of relaxation, he went to Ford's Theater on April 14, where he was shot from behind by a Confederate supporter, actor **John Wilkes Booth**. Taken to a home across the street where doctors rushed to his side, Lincoln died the next morning. With his passing, something went out of the American political spirit, a genuineness and human appeal that has never since been equaled.

P. T. Barnum

Phineas Taylor Barnum, the man who designed and promoted "**The Greatest Show on Earth,**" was born in Bethel, Connecticut in 1810.

At the age of 25, he moved to New York City and came across an elderly African-American slave named Joice Heth. Barnum accepted Heth's claim that she was 161 years old and had served as George Washington's nurse. He bought her from her master and on August 10, 1835, he held the first of what became numerous receptions for Heth in Niblo's Garden in New York City.

The death of his protégé, Heth, did not deter Barnum, who had recognized his great gift for publicity and promotion. In 1841, he bought Scudder's American Museum at the corner of Broadway and Ann streets. The resulting **Barnum's American Museum** became the showplace for Barnum's second great performer, a five-year-old midget

"General Tom Thumb." Barnum took Tom Thumb to England in 1844. The British aristocracy was charmed by the midget, and Barnum's prestige grew. Upon his return to America, Barnum soon built "Iranistan," an Oriental-style palace in Bridgeport, Connecticut.

In 1850, Barnum served as host and promoter to the "Swedish Nightingale," Jenny Lind, who gave 95 concerts in 19 American cities. Barnum earned $535,000 from the tour. Barnum embarked on another European tour with Tom Thumb and Cordelia Howard (who played "Little Eva" in the popular play *Uncle Tom's Cabin*). He began to exhibit hippopotami, white whales, Indian chiefs, and even the celebrated marriage of Tom Thumb to Lavinia Warren (another midget) on February 10, 1863.

In 1871, Barnum joined forces with William C. Coup and the two men organized the **Great Traveling World's Fair**, which opened in Brooklyn, New York on April 10, 1871. Barnum later broke with Coup and joined James A. Bailey in creating the **Barnum and Bailey Greatest Show on Earth**. The height of the circus' success came in 1882 when Barnum purchased and brought from England, "Jumbo," a six-and-a-half-ton African elephant. "Jumbo-mania" prevailed in the United States, and Barnum, who spent $30,000 in purchase and transportation fees, earned $336,000 in box office receipts in the first six weeks after the animal's arrival.

Jumbo was run down in a locomotive accident in Ontario, Canada in 1885, but Barnum quickly imported a female elephant that became known as "Jumbo's widow." Barnum brought his entire circus to England for one last international tour in 1889. He died two years later, leaving an estate of $4.3 million.

36. Harriet Beecher Stowe
(1811–1896)

One of nine children born to Reverend Lyman Beecher (1775–1863) and Roxanna Foote, **Harriet Beecher Stowe** was raised in Lichfield, Connecticut. The Beecher family was perhaps the most doggedly intellectual, religious and progressive household in early 19th century America. Her father was the foremost Puritan preacher of his generation, three of her brothers became prominent ministers, and her sister, Catharine, founded the private school for women in Hartford, Connecticut that Harriet herself attended.

The family moved to Cincinnati, Ohio in 1832. Harriet taught there, and in 1836, married Calvin E. Stowe, a faculty member at Lane Theological Seminary. Harriet Beecher Stowe raised a family during the 1830s and 1840s. She underwent incredible grief when her sixth child died of cholera in 1849. Later she declared it was in the moment of the child's burial that she felt for the first time the searing pain African-American women must have felt when their family members were taken from them by the relentless system of slavery. Separated only by the Ohio River from a slave-holding community, Stowe traveled in the south and developed firm convictions about the immorality of the slave system.

In 1850, she and her family moved to Brunswick, Maine (her husband had a new appointment at Bowdoin College), and it was there that she wrote *Uncle Tom's Cabin, or, Life Among the Lowly*, which was first published in serial form in the *National Era*, a Washington, D.C. anti-slavery newspaper. The story came out in book form in 1852, and within one year's time it had sold 300,000 copies. Slavery became a hotter issue than ever before, and Harriet Beecher Stowe was an immediate celebrity (at least in the north). When she later met **Abraham Lincoln** (see no. 34), he exclaimed, "So you're

Harriet Beecher Stowe

the little woman who wrote the book that made this great war!" Stowe later wrote *The Key to Uncle Tom's Cabin* (1853) and *Dred: A Tale of the Great Dismal Swamp* (1856).

She went to Europe in 1853 and was lionized by English society; her writing had in fact made an enormous impact upon the British working classes, which remained staunchly pro-north throughout the **Civil War**. Although her most important work was by far her anti-slavery writing, Stowe also wrote numerous works of fiction, biography and children's literature before her death in 1896.

Stephen Douglas
(1813–1861)

The "Little Giant" who introduced the calamitous **Kansas-Nebraska Act** to Congress was originally from New England. Born in Brandon, Vermont, **Stephen A. Douglas** became a westerner by choice. In January 1833, the 19-year-old Douglas went west.

Douglas settled in Jacksonville, Illinois. He was soon admitted to the bar in Illinois and pinned his fortunes to those of the rising Democratic Party, thereby elevating himself to the level of judge on the state Supreme Court by the age of 27. He served briefly as secretary of state for Illinois (1840) and in the U.S. House of Representatives (1843–1847).

He rose rapidly in Congress, winning election to the U.S. Senate in 1846 and served as senator until his death. In 1852, he tried to gain the Democratic nomination for president.

Failing in this, he then used his influence as chairperson of the Senate Committee on Territories to introduce on January 4, 1854, the **Kansas-Nebraska Act**, which would organize both of those territories as states. The act ignited a storm of controversy, since the **Missouri Compromise** of 1820 had forbidden the introduction of slavery north of the line drawn at 36 degrees, 30 minutes of latitude. Douglas prevailed in shepherding the bill through Congress. Douglas asserted that "**popular sovereignty**" should decide whether slavery could or could not be introduced into the new territories.

The Kansas-Nebraska Act brought the slavery issue to a head and gave birth, inadvertently, to the new Republican Party in 1856. One of its prominent members who was also from Illinois, **Abraham Lincoln** (see no. 34), challenged Douglas for his Senate seat in 1858. The **Lincoln-Douglas Debates** (held between August 21 and October 15) marked the height of stump speaking in 19th century politics. Only five feet tall, Douglas neverthe-

Stephen Douglas

less projected well with his voice, while Lincoln impressed many with his subtle arguments. At a time when the north and south were at growing odds, Douglas tried to orient Americans to the west. He saw America's future as lying beyond the Mississippi River. Douglas received fewer popular votes in the election than Lincoln, but the state's apportionment of representatives threw the election to Douglas.

After his term as senator had ended, Douglas ran for president as the nominee of the northern Democrats in 1860. Coming in a distant second to Lincoln, who was the Republican nominee, he then gave all his support to the new president and the cause of keeping the Union together. He approved when Lincoln called for volunteers to fight the war, and went on a tour of speaking engagements in support of the new administration. Stricken with typhoid fever, he died at the age of 48.

38. John Fremont
(1813–1890)

Known as the "Pathfinder" to two generations of Americans, **John Fremont** was born in Savannah, Georgia. Fremont's first job was teaching mathematics on a naval sloop that sailed around South America. He surveyed for the railroad to be built in Tennessee and was commissioned second lieutenant in the U.S. Topographical Corps in 1838.

Fremont obtained command of an important exploratory expedition during 1842. Using scout **Kit Carson** as a guide, Fremont and his men charted the Wind River area in present-day Wyoming. This was followed by a second expedition (1843–1844) during which Fremont led federal explorers up the Arkansas River and on to the Great Salt Lake, all the way to Fort Vancouver in the Oregon Territory (now Vancouver, Washington). They returned by way of the Sierra Nevada. Fremont's return to St. Louis, Missouri, and the ensuing report he wrote on the expedition, ignited a wave of excitement about the American west. From that time on, he was called the "Pathfinder."

Fremont led a third expedition (1845–1846), which brought him to northern California at the start of the **Mexican War**. He and his men participated in the **Bear Flag Revolt**, which ousted the Mexicans and set up a new republic in California. Unfortunately, in the confusion that followed, Fremont obeyed the orders of Commodore **Robert F. Stockton** rather than those of General **Stephen W. Kearny**. Taken by Kearny to Washington, D.C., Fremont was tried by court-martial and found guilty of mutiny and disobedience. Although President **James K. Polk** (see no. 28) rescinded the prescribed punishment, Fremont chose to resign from the army.

Fremont spent the 1850s in California and served as senator from 1850–1851. In 1856, the newly formed Republican Party nominated him for president. Both Fremont and his opponent, Democrat **James Buchanan**, conducted lackluster, even half-hearted campaigns, but Buchanan won by 174 electoral votes to 114 .

When the **Civil War** began in 1861, **Abraham Lincoln** (see no. 34) named Fremont commander of the Department of the West, with headquarters in St. Louis. Fremont prematurely freed all the slaves in Missouri and was removed from command in December 1861. Although he received another assignment, command of the Mountain Division in present-day West Virginia, Fremont again resigned from the army in 1864.

He held one last appointment, governor of the Territory of Arizona (1878–1883). In 1890, Congress made Fremont a major general and placed him on the pension list just prior to his death that year in New York City.

John Fremont

Frederick Douglass
(1817–1895)

Frederick Douglass

The most prominent African-American of the 19th century was born a slave near Easton in Talbot County, Maryland. The son of a slave woman and, most likely, her white master, **Frederick Douglass** was christened Frederick Augustus Washington Bailey. Determined to elevate himself and improve his fortunes, he escaped September 3, 1838, and made his way north to New York City.

He soon changed his name to Frederick Douglass, in emulation of the hero in Sir Walter Scott's poem *The Lady of the Lake*. He made his first appearance at an antislavery society lecture in 1841 and almost immediately became a spokesperson for **William Lloyd Garrison**'s Massachusetts Antislavery Society. Four years of successful presentations followed. When many people questioned whether his story was true (for how could an ex-slave show such dignity, strength and composure?) he wrote and published *Narrative of the Life of Frederick Douglass* (1845).

Douglass went to the British Isles, where he remained for two years. Treated for the first time in his life as a true equal, he developed strong friendships with Britons, who purchased his freedom from his former master, Thomas Auld, of Maryland. Douglass returned to the United States a free man and began to publish the *North Star*, which later was changed to *Frederick Douglass's Paper*, and then, the *Douglass Monthly*.

Douglass became progressively more radical during the 1850s. He supported **John Brown**'s efforts to free slaves (see no. 29) and came to believe that only a violent clash could free the country from the grip of slavery. He welcomed the start of the **Civil War** in 1861, seeing it as the second phase of the American Revolution, a struggle that had begun, but would not be finished until liberty was won for *all* people.

He criticized the Lincoln administration for its emphasis on the Union rather than on slavery, and was gratified when Lincoln issued the **Emancipation Proclamation**, thereby identifying the war as a two-part struggle: for the Union, and, for the freedom of slaves. Douglass was one of the recruiters for the all-black Massachusetts 54th Regiment, and he became an important adviser to Lincoln in the last two years of his presidency.

Loyal to the Republican Party, he was rewarded with a series of appointments. He served as marshal for the District of Columbia (1877–1881), as recorder of deeds for the district (1881–1886) and as U.S. minister to Haiti (1889–1891).

Douglass had been the single most outspoken and noteworthy African-American of the 19th century. His complex legacy of leadership was transferred after his death to two other remarkable men, **W. E. B. Du Bois** (see no. 65) and **Booker T. Washington** (see no. 56).

40. Allan Pinkerton
(1819–1884)

The grandfather of all private detectives, **Allan Pinkerton** was born in Glasgow, Scotland. When he was 12 years old, his father, a jail guard, died of injuries suffered on the job. Apprenticed to a cooper (a barrel-maker), Pinkerton became active in the Chartist movement, which sought to extend voting rights in Great Britain. In order to escape arrest for his Chartist activities, in 1842, Pinkerton embarked on a ship bound for Canada with Joan Carfrae, whom he married one day before the departure.

Surviving a shipwreck and reaching Canada, the couple settled in Illinois. Pinkerton opened a cooperage of his own in Dundee, Illinois, but found he was irresistibly drawn to detective work. His investigations led to the arrest of a notorious counterfeiter, and he soon became a deputy sheriff in Cook County, Illinois. He set up the first private detective agency in the United States in Chicago (1850), became a special agent for the U.S. Mail service (1853), and on February 1, 1855, received a contract to protect several railroad lines from bomb threats and disturbances.

In 1861, Pinkerton discovered a plot to assassinate President-elect **Abraham Lincoln** (see no. 34) on his way through Baltimore, Maryland. Pinkerton's warning persuaded Lincoln to bypass Baltimore, and although many scholars since then have insisted Pinkerton had little evidence to work with, the incident served to strengthen Pinkerton's name and reputation. In 1861 and 1862, he served with the **Army of the Potomac** (which was created to capture the Confederate capital of Richmond) under the assumed name and title of Major E. J. Allen. His investigations of Confederate troop placements gave a great deal of vital information to General **George B. McClellan** who was usually too cautious a leader to employ the data available to him. Pinkerton left the army in November 1862 when McClellan was replaced.

He established branch offices of his agency in Philadelphia and New York before a paralytic stroke (1869) left him at only half his usual strength. From that time on, he left the field investigations to others and concentrated on the coordination and command of his detectives. In his later years, Pinkerton wrote 18 volumes of detective narratives, starting an entire genre in American literature. Two of his sons took over the agency after his death.

Allan Pinkerton (l) with Lincoln & McClellan

The most determined and powerful suffragette of the 19th century, **Susan B. Anthony** was born in the manufacturing town of Adams, Massachusetts. Her Quaker parents moved the family to upstate New York where Anthony grew up on the family farm. She went into teaching and became headmistress of Canajoharie Academy (1845–1848). Anthony returned to the family farm in 1848, where she learned about the first women's rights convention in Seneca Falls, New York which her parents had recently attended.

Having been raised by Quakers who believed in the essential equality of the genders, Anthony was soon attracted to the growing movement for women's rights. She met **Elizabeth Cady Stanton** for the first time in 1850. The older woman became a mentor as well as friend. Anthony labored between 1850 and 1860 to bring about change in New York state. Her success was noted by the passage of the state **Married Women's Property Act** (1860), which gave married women the right to their own earnings and the right to sue in court. At the same time, she served as the chief agent for **William Lloyd Garrison**'s Anti-Slavery Society in New York state, collecting thousands of signatures calling for emancipation of the slaves.

Anthony was greatly disturbed when the U.S. Congress passed the **Fifteenth Amendment** to the **Constitution**, guaranteeing the right to vote to all citizens "regardless of race or color," but not including women. She then formed the **American Equal Rights Association** (1866) and published a suffrage paper, *The Revolution* (1868–1870).

Anthony directed the first woman suffrage convention, held in Washington, D.C. in 1869. Her efforts to win equality for women at the national level were opposed by a group led by **Lucy Stone**; the minority group called for a state-by-state effort. The result was a

Susan B. Anthony

split in the ranks that led to Anthony leading the new National Woman Suffrage Association and Stone directing the new American Woman Suffrage Association. The two leaders reconciled in 1890, and the reunited group was called the **National American Woman Suffrage Association**. Anthony was president of the association from 1892 to 1900.

Anthony had the joy of seeing the right of women to vote first guaranteed in Wyoming Territory (1870), and then, in the state of Wyoming (1890). She campaigned fiercely in South Dakota, but was defeated by the liquor interests, which persuaded the populace that female suffrage would lead to the prohibition of liquor.

She became revered by the press and the general populace at the turn of the century. She yielded her post as head of the suffrage association to **Carrie Chapman Catt** (1859–1947) in 1900. Anthony attended her last suffrage convention in 1906 and uttered the famous words, "Failure is impossible." She died that year, 14 years before the **Nineteenth Amendment** (called by many the "Anthony Amendment") gave women throughout the United States the right to vote.

Mary Baker Eddy
(1821–1910)

The only major American religious denomination to be founded by a woman, **Christian Science**, grew out of the life struggles of **Mary Baker Eddy**, born as Mary Morse Baker in 1821 in Bow, New Hampshire. Suffering poor health, she stayed mostly at home in her youth and was tutored by one of her older brothers. By her late teens, she had rejected the stern Calvinistic faith of her father and searched for years for a set of beliefs to provide the moral certainty not found during her youth.

In 1862, she sought help for her physical and psychological ills by visiting the healer Phineas Quimby in Portland, Maine. She came away from her meetings with a new belief in the "science of health," which persuaded her that the cause of physical illness lay in the mind.

This belief was reinforced four years later after she was critically injured by a fall. Reading the Bible, she was struck by these words in Matthew 9:1–8: "But that you may know that the Son of Man has power on earth to forgive sins" (then he said to the paralytic) "Arise, take up thy pallet and go to thy house." Eddy became even more convinced of the power of the mind over the body. From that time on, until the end of her life, Eddy was fully involved in reading, writing, studying and teaching about her beliefs, which she crystallized in the book *Science and Health with Key to the Scriptures* (1875). The volume was reissued no fewer than 382 times during her own lifetime and had an enormous effect on the public.

She founded the Christian Scientists Association in 1876. The name was changed in 1879 to the **Church of Christ Scientist**, and was reorganized into the format it maintains today. In 1877, she married Asa Gilbert Eddy, a sewing-machine salesperson who became a valued assistant in spreading her beliefs. She founded the *Christian Science Monitor* newspaper in 1908 and died at Chestnut Hill, Massachusetts in 1910. At the time of her death there were nearly 100,000 members of the church she had founded.

Eddy's beliefs that illness and disease are created in the mind was by no means original, but the manner in which she put the idea across, and the energy with which she invested her new denomination, gave new meaning to the concept of self-will.

Mary Baker Eddy

43. Clara Barton
(1821–1912)

Clara Barton was born in Oxford, Massachusetts in 1821 as Clarissa Barton. She taught in neighboring schools and moved to New Jersey, where she founded the state's first free school in 1852. During the 1850s, she went to Washington, D.C., where she took a job in the **U.S. Patent Office**.

At the start of the **Civil War**, Barton witnessed the appalling lack of first aid available to the wounded and dying after the Battle of Bull Run. She advertised for volunteers and supplies and opened her living quarters as a storeroom for bandages, medicine and food. By the summer of 1862, she had begun to distribute the supplies by mule team to both hospitals and battlefields. Known to many soldiers as the "Angel of the Battlefield," she was present at the battles of **Cedar Mountain**, **Second Bull Run**, **Chantilly**, **South Mountain**, **Antietam**, and **Fredericksburg**. Adaptive and cooperative, Barton was nonetheless always in control of the situation; she stayed firmly independent of the **U.S. Sanitary Commission** and **Dorothea Dix**'s women nurses (see no. 31).

As the role of the Sanitary Commission grew, Barton found less need for her services on the battlefield, and in June 1864, she became head nurse for General **Benjamin Butler**'s (1818–1893) Army of the James. In February 1865, she began the laborious, though painfully necessary, task of preparing lists of the thousands of men who were missing in action; her work led to the identification of many Union soldiers who had died while imprisoned in the notorious prison camp at Andersonville, Georgia.

For three years following the war, Barton delivered lectures around the country based on her wartime experiences. She suffered an attack of nervous exhaustion in 1868 and went to Europe for rest. There she learned for the first time of the International Committee of the Red Cross, which had been given official status by many nations in 1864 — but not by the United States.

She returned to nursing during the Franco-Prussian War in Europe (1870–1871) and then returned home, where she began to campaign for American acceptance of the Red Cross. Many Americans felt that signing the Red Cross treaty would violate the principles of the **Monroe Doctrine**, but Barton pressed forward, and in 1882, President **Chester A. Arthur** signed the treaty.

Barton organized the **American Association of the Red Cross** in 1881. She spent the next 23 years directing relief efforts both in the United States and abroad.

Clara Barton

The most prolific landscape architect of his generation, **Frederick Law Olmsted** was born in Hartford, Connecticut to upper-class parents. By the time he was 16, Olmsted had already made four 1,000-plus-mile journeys with his family and had developed what became a lasting love of outdoor life. In 1843, he boarded a merchant ship for China. The one-year round-trip voyage convinced him more than ever that the active, outdoor life was the one most worth living.

Olmsted engaged in gentleman farming (1847–1850) before he embarked on a series of journeys (1850–1856) that took him to England, continental Europe and the American South. Having observed the system of slavery up close, he condensed his journal notes into *The Cotton Kingdom* (two volumes, 1861), which gave a revealing and informed portrait of the south. Olmsted then traveled to Italy, where he was inspired to undertake landscape architecture, and in 1857, he was named superintendent of the soon-to-be-constructed **Central Park** in New York City. Working closely with English architect Calvert Vaux, Olmsted became architect-in-chief for the park that became a model for open spaces in North America.

Olmsted took a leave of absence from Central Park in 1861 to accept appointment as general secretary of the U.S. Sanitary Commission. He resigned that post in 1863 and went west to supervise the Fremont Marisposa mining estates in California. While there, Olmsted fell in love with the **Yosemite** valley in California's **Sierra Nevada** and had the satisfaction of seeing it become a state park. (Yosemite became a national park in 1890.) He also designed the grounds of the **University of California at Berkeley**.

Olmsted returned to New York City in 1865 and proceeded to design **Riverside Park**; then he designed Chicago's **South**

Frederick Olmsted

Park. He took over the leadership of the Boston park system in 1875. When Olmsted retired in 1895, he had left his mark on more than 80 public parks and grounds, including the **U.S. Capitol** in Washington, D.C.; Mount Royal Park in Montreal, Quebec; the New York State capitol, in Albany; **Belle Isle Park** in Detroit, Michigan, and, perhaps most important, the **World's Fair** at Chicago in 1890.

Combining the artistic courage of a dreamer with the practical vision of a planner, Olmsted changed the way Americans viewed open space, and many had been converted to his view that open spaces need to be preserved for the good of the public, as a resource for all.

Ulysses S. Grant

Ulysses Simpson Grant was one of the most dogged and intrepid generals in American warfare. Born Hiram Ulysses Grant, he found on arrival at the **U.S. Military Academy at West Point** that the congressman who appointed him had accidentally given his name as Ulysses Simpson Grant. He graduated in 1843 and was made a second lieutenant.

He served with distinction in the **Mexican War**. In 1852, an army assignment took him to Fort Vancouver in present-day Washington State. He resigned from the army as a captain (1854) and tried farming (1854–1858) and then real estate (1858–1860). Having failed in each enterprise, he was working at his father's leather shop when the **Civil War** began in 1861.

Grant organized a volunteer unit and soon rose to the rank of brigadier general of volunteers. He proved his mettle in February 1862 with the brilliant capture of Confederate forts **Donelson** and **Henry**. When the Confederate commander of Fort Donelson asked for terms of negotiation, Grant responded tersely that "No terms except unconditional and immediate surrender can be accepted." Hence, the nickname, "Unconditional Surrender" (U.S.) Grant. He fought the Confederates to a draw at **Shiloh** and led the Army of the West on a brilliant campaign of marching and countermarching. He completely outmaneuvered the enemy, leading to the surrender of **Vicksburg** on the east bank of the Mississippi River in July 1863.

Named commander of the Union Armies in 1864, Grant engaged Confederate general **Robert E. Lee** in a series of grueling and bloody battles in Virginia. Remorseless, Grant pursued the campaign and siege of Richmond and Petersburg until the Confederates withdrew in the spring of 1865. Pursuing rapidly, Grant caught up with the enemy, and on April 9, 1865, Lee surrendered his sword to Grant at **Appomattox Court House** in Virginia.

As the conquering hero of the Civil War, Grant easily won election to the presidency in 1868 and 1872. He was, unfortunately, no politician; he appointed friends to high posts and maintained them there even when it became obvious they were untrustworthy. Grant's loyalty, which had served him so well in wartime, worked against him as president. Grant left the presidency in 1877 and went on a two-year world tour. Abroad, he was greeted by foreigners as the Civil War hero rather than as a failed president.

The last years of his life were financially difficult. Grant was forced to sell his swords and souvenirs. Knowing that he had cancer of the throat, he raced to complete his *Personal Memoirs* before his death. Published posthumously by **Mark Twain** (see no. 48), the memoirs were immensely popular and provided $450,000 in royalties for his family.

46. Sitting Bull
(1831–1890)

The spiritual and military leader of the Sioux nation was born on the Grand River in present-day South Dakota as Tatanka Iyotake. **Sitting Bull** was nicknamed "Slow" in his youth for his deliberate manner of action. He fought his first battle against Crow Indians at the age of 14. Both resolute and cunning in warfare, Sitting Bull became the leader of the Strong Heart Warrior Society around 1856, and by 1867, he was the leader of the entire **Sioux nation**.

Like many great Native American leaders before him — **King Philip**, **Pontiac** and **Tecumseh** (see no. 18) — Sitting Bull needed to inspire and persuade his men to fight. The fact that Sitting Bull was able to organize the resources and energy of the Sioux nation is a testament to his oratorical powers. Early in June 1876, Sitting Bull and Chief **Crazy Horse** (see no. 53) gathered 1,800 warriors in South Dakota and held a sun dance, where Sitting Bull had a profound vision of American soldiers falling dead and wounded to the ground. His oracular powers seemed to be confirmed on June 25, when the Sioux warriors surrounded and destroyed the entire Seventh Cavalry unit led by Lieutenant Colonel **George Armstrong Custer** in the spectacular Native American victory at the Little Bighorn in present-day Montana.

The Sioux victory was short-lived. Thousands of U.S. infantry and cavalry poured into present-day North Dakota, South Dakota and Montana. Sitting Bull crossed the border into Canada in May 1877 to receive the protection of "Grandmother Victoria" (Queen Victoria of England). After negotiations between the United States and Great Britain, he returned to the United States and officially surrendered at Fort Buford on July 19, 1881.

Confined to the **Standing Rock Indian Reservation** in North Dakota, Sitting Bull remained there until 1885, when he signed a contract to tour with **Buffalo Bill Cody**'s Wild West Show (he received $50 a week plus a $125 signing bonus).

Sitting Bull returned to the reservation the next year and remained there while a new religious fervor swept the Sioux Indians in 1890, the "Ghost Dance," a blend of Christianity and traditional Native American beliefs. This movement was seen as a threat because of the militant history of the Sioux. Mistakenly believing that Sitting Bull had engineered the new tumult, the U.S. Army decided to apprehend the aged Sioux chief. On December 15, 1890, he was arrested by agents of the Office of Indian Affairs and was shot and killed in a scuffle immediately following the arrest.

Sitting Bull

Andrew Carnegie

If ever an American personified the twin virtues of making a fortune and then giving it away, that man was **Andrew Carnegie**. Born in Dunfermline, Scotland, Carnegie came to the United States in 1848 when his family moved to Allegheny, Pennsylvania.

Carnegie's first job was in a cotton factory, where he labored for $1.20 a week. He then obtained work as a clerk, while attending night school, and in 1850 he became a messenger boy for the telegraph office in Pittsburgh, Pennsylvania. Carnegie rose to become a relief telegraph operator and then a regular operator. His diligence caught the eye of **Thomas Scott**, division superintendent of the Pennsylvania Railroad. Scott quickly hired Carnegie as his personal clerk and telegraph operator; from that point on, Carnegie

ascended rapidly in business. By 1859, he became chief superintendent of the Pittsburgh division of the railroad.

During the Civil War years, Carnegie made investments that paid off handsomely. He was able to resign from the railroad in 1865 and enter the new iron industry. By 1868, he was earning an average of $50,000 a year. Then he began to obtain rights to processes key to the iron industry. He had the first **Lucy Furnace** built in America (1870), and by 1877, his industrial furnaces were used in manufacturing one-seventh of all the **Bessemer-processed** steel in the United States.

Carnegie brought in **Henry Clay Frick** (1849–1919) as his assistant to run the steel mills in Homestead, Pennsylvania. A major strike took place in 1892. Carnegie fully supported Frick's use of force and bloodshed to end the strike. This black mark against Carnegie's name did not hinder the continued growth of his business. In 1896, he obtained a favorable lease on the Mesabi iron-ore mines in Minnesota, which allowed for even greater expansion of his enterprises. He reorganized his affairs under the title of **Carnegie Steel Company** in 1899. In 1901, he sold all his holdings to financier **J. P. Morgan** (see no. 49) for $250 million in bonds in the newly-created company, **U.S. Steel**.

Having become one of the richest people in America, Carnegie proceeded to give away much that he had earned. He expressed his ideas about charity in *The Gospel of Wealth* (1900), and gave approximately $350 million to public libraries, the **Carnegie Foundation for the Advancement of Teaching**, the **Carnegie Institution of Washington** and the **Carnegie Hero Funds**. Certainly the greatest philanthropist of his day, a true idealist and a tough businessman, Carnegie was a symbol of much that was acclaimed and derided during the **Gilded Age** (1870–1914) of America.

48. Mark Twain
(1835–1910)

Mark Twain, the best-loved American humorist, was born Samuel Langhorne Clemens in Florida, Missouri. He grew up along the banks of the Mississippi River and in his twenties became a pilot for steamboats on the great and muddy river. The start of the **Civil War** closed the river to passenger traffic and Clemens enrolled in the Confederate army, where he remained for only two weeks (he would later refer to having "resigned," but it was unquestionably an act of desertion).

Clemens traveled west to Nevada and tried his hand at prospecting for gold and silver. Failing in that, he went to work as a journalist for the Virginia City (Nevada) *Territorial Enterprise*. By February 1863, he had begun to sign his articles with "Mark Twain," which was a steamboat pilot's term for water that was two fathoms deep. The pen name stuck.

After a rival journalist threatened him to a duel, Twain went to San Francisco and then the California countryside, where he wrote *The Celebrated Jumping Frog of Calaveras County* in 1865. He soon departed the west and went to New York City, where he worked for the *Saturday Press*. Following a voyage to Europe and the Middle East (1867), he wrote his first major book, *The Innocents Abroad* (1869), which became popular with the American public. Twain worked briefly as the editor of the *Buffalo Express* before he settled in Hartford, Connecticut.

He proceeded to write a number of humorous works, including *Roughing It* (1872) and *The Gilded Age* (1873). Twain then wrote his most successful books, *The Adventures of Tom Sawyer* (1876) and *The Adventures of Huckleberry Finn* (1884), both of which drew on his boyhood years in Missouri. *The Prince and the Pauper* (1882) and *A Connecticut Yankee in King Arthur's Court* (1889) further endeared him to the reading public, in part due to his skillful con-trast of American and European cultural values.

He invested in a project to build a type-setting machine that nearly bankrupted him because it was never completed. Forced to sell his impressive Hartford home, Twain spent his last years in Redding, Connecticut. The great literary value of his work was first, a clarity of style, and second, that he liberated humor from the straitjacketed approach it had previously had in American literature.

Mark Twain

The most powerful financier in America was **John Pierpont Morgan**. Born in Hartford, Connecticut, he was the oldest of five children. His merchant father was named to head a banking branch in London in 1853, and so Morgan left the Boston school system and studied in Switzerland, and then, at the University of Gottingen in Germany, where his chief study was in mathematics.

In 1857, Morgan entered business as an accountant with the New York City banking firm of **Duncan, Sherman & Co.**, which served as the U.S. agent for **George Peabody & Co.** in England, the firm his father was associated with. Morgan was promoted to become the New York agent for his father's firm, and in 1864, he joined **Dabney, Morgan & Co.** in New York. Further changes over the years altered the name to **Drexel, Morgan & Co.** (1871–1893), and finally, **J. P. Morgan & Co.** (1895).

Morgan's first great business coup came in 1879 when he unloaded $25 million worth of **Vanderbilt** railroad stock in England (to a profit of $3 million for his firm). His extensive business connections in London proved immeasurably important in the late 19th century, when new American businesses and the American federal government required large amounts of capital. Morgan floated loans from England and profited greatly from his position as the number-one source of gold for the U.S. government. In 1895, he acquired $65 million in gold for the government and thereby saved the U.S. Treasury from the embarrassment of having to suspend the redemption of currency in gold coin. Morgan made a good profit from the transaction, which increased his wealth and prestige.

In 1901, Morgan brokered the agreement that led to a merger of companies to form the first billion-dollar corporation, **U.S. Steel**. He averted a widespread financial collapse in

J. P. Morgan

1907 following a panic on Wall Street. By 1910, there was no question that the "House of Morgan" (as his many financial interests in currency, railroads and finance were called) controlled the lion's share of wealth in New York City.

Morgan's very success led to changes in the financial system. Seeing that so much power had devolved into the hands of one banking house, Congress called for, and received, the development of the **Federal Reserve System** in 1913, an institution that would monitor Wall Street developments.

Morgan died in Rome, Italy in 1913, unaware of the extent to which government regulation would change finance in the future. He left an enormous fortune, as well as the greatest private collection of art in North America.

50. John Muir
(1838–1914)

The third of eight children, **John Muir** was born in Dunbar, Scotland. In 1849, his father took three of the children to Wisconsin, and the rest of the family followed soon after.

Muir attended the University of Wisconsin from 1860 to 1863, but he left without a degree. Having studied chemistry and geology, he tinkered with mechanical inventions at first, but in 1867, he embarked on what would be his life passion — exploring the wilderness, writing about his discoveries and persuading others to join him in a new quest to preserve the American wilderness.

Muir walked from Indiana to the Gulf of Mexico in 1867. His observations of flora and fauna on the journey were assembled much later and published as *A Thousand Mile Walk to the Gulf* (1916).

He then traveled to the far west and spent the years 1868 through 1874 in the vicinity of the **Yosemite** valley in California. His observations led him to conclude that the valley, and its unique features, had been formed by glacial erosion. He then meandered in Nevada, Utah and the American northwest before journeying to Alaska for the first time in 1879. There he discovered **Glacier Bay** and the glacier that was later named for him.

Muir married Louise Strentzel in 1880. He purchased part of the Strentzel family fruit ranch from his father-in-law and turned to horticulture for the next 10 years (1881–1891). During that decade he earned enough money to provide for both his own basic needs (which to him, meant the ability to be free to travel) and the material well-being of his wife and two daughters.

Muir went north to Alaska again, to discover and describe in his writings, many Alaskan glaciers. During the period of horticultural work, he laid the groundwork that led Congress to establish the Sequoia and Yosemite national parks in 1890. Muir founded the **Sierra Club** (1892), which was devoted to the preservation of wilderness.

Perhaps most important was Muir's friendship and association with President **Theodore Roosevelt** (see no. 58). The former rancher had a strong interest in wilderness areas, and Muir used their friendship to the advantage of the forests of the American west. In 1897, Muir wrote articles for *Harper's Weekly* and *Atlantic Monthly* that turned the tide of public opinion toward conservation. Other important publications included *The Mountains of California* (1894) and *Our National Parks* (1901). Largely as a result of Muir's efforts, President Roosevelt set aside 148 million acres of forest reserves between 1901 and 1909.

John Muir (r) with Teddy Roosevelt

51. John D. Rockefeller
(1839–1937)

One of the most profoundly inspiring stories of rags-to-riches is that of **John Davison Rockefeller**, born the son of a peddler in Richford, New York. His family moved to Cleveland, Ohio when Rockefeller was 14; he went to work two years later as a clerk on a small produce farm. He worked his way up and soon bought a partnership in a grain commission house. Deeply religious from an early age, he gave 10 percent of his earnings to churches.

The first oil well was drilled in Pennsylvania in 1859 by **Edwin Drake**. Seeing the potential for growth in this new industry, Rockefeller formed a partnership and organized **Andrews, Clark & Co.** in 1863. It has been said that Rockefeller's greatest passion was for organization and efficiency; these qualities certainly formed the basis for his manner of handling the oil business. Seeking to create a unified flow of oil from producer to consumer, Rockefeller created **Standard Oil Company** in 1870 and managed to gain a near-monopoly of the refineries in Cleveland, New York, Pittsburgh and Philadelphia. In 1882, Rockefeller organized **Standard Oil Trust**, which took over control of production and transportation from Standard Oil Company, and soon came to control much of the world trade in oil.

This success attracted criticism in the newspapers from people who feared Rockefeller's economic power, and a major court case was brought before the Ohio Supreme Court (1891–1892). In 1892, the court dissolved the trust under the provisions of the **Sherman Antitrust Act**. Rockefeller and his associates accepted the court's ruling that all their companies had to operate independently of one another, but their ingenious response was to form a holding company, Standard Oil Company of New Jersey. Therefore, even though Rockefeller himself

John D. Rockefeller

retired in 1895, his holding company continued to maintain a near-monopoly. Seeing this, the federal government brought another suit (1906–1911) against the holding company, and in 1911, the U.S. Supreme Court ruled the company had to be dissolved.

None of this legal activity impeded Rockefeller's success. He lived on three different estates, and proceeded to give nearly $500 million to foundations and organizations during his later years. During the last 20 years of his life, Rockefeller was seen as the epitome of American success, a poor boy who had come to greatness and remembered to give generously of his wealth.

Critics would charge he established a pattern of monopoly that would come to dominate American business in the 20th century. His admirers would counter that monopolies were sometimes needed to introduce efficiency in an industry.

Born in 1841, in Boston, Massachusetts, **Oliver Wendell Holmes, Jr.** was the son of a renowned poet and essayist. He found delight in his New England heritage and loved Boston, with its monuments and plaques that echoed a glorious past.

He graduated from Harvard College in 1861, the same year the **Civil War** began, and he enlisted in the northern army. During his military service he was wounded at **Ball's Bluff**, **Antietam** and **Fredericksburg**. He left the service with the rank of lieutenant colonel.

Holmes graduated from Harvard Law School in 1866 and was admitted to the bar in 1867. He was co-editor of the *American Law Review,* and in 1881 published *The Common Law,* which was to be his finest written work, although he had not yet served as a judge. In 1882, he was appointed, first as a professor of law at Harvard and then to the Supreme Judicial Court of Massachusetts, where he served until 1902.

Holmes was elevated to chief justice of the Massachusetts supreme court in 1899, and in 1902, President **Theodore Roosevelt** (see no. 58) appointed him as an associate justice of the **U.S. Supreme Court**. Holmes went to Washington, D.C. in 1902 and served on the Court until 1932.

During his 30-year presence on the Supreme Court, Holmes became known as the "**Great Dissenter**." He dissented in key decisions such as *Lochner v. New York* (1905), which stated that a law limiting bakery employees to a 10-hour work day was unconstitutional, and *Adkins v. Children's Hospital* (1923), which struck down a minimum-wage law in the District of Columbia. In dissenting, Holmes argued that in both cases the laws in question were reasonable attempts on the part of legislatures to regulate working conditions for employees.

In 1916, **Louis D. Brandeis** joined the Court as an associate justice. He and Holmes concurred in many of their opinions and their frequent dissents from the majority led to them being identified as the defenders of liberal principles on the traditionally conservative Court. This distinction was not completely accurate.

Holmes felt the Court had limited powers, particularly concerning the interpretation of "due process of law," which he believed should not be applied to economic rulings. Holmes, however, was not a typical liberal. He admired successful men of business and was as close to a true aristocrat as any American could be. One of his greatest judicial contributions was the development of the concept that only a "clear and present danger" to civil law could permit the suppression of free speech. Both as a philosopher and as a judge, Holmes believed the law needed to evolve along with the society it served.

Holmes resigned his position in 1932, at the age of 91. He died at 93 and was buried at Arlington National Cemetery.

Oliver Wendell Holmes, Jr.

"Ho-Kay dey! It is a good day to fight! It is a good day to die! Strong hearts, brave hearts to the front! Weak hearts and cowards to the rear." With these stirring words, the **Oglala Sioux** chief, **Crazy Horse**, led both Sioux and **Cheyenne** warriors in the charges that overwhelmed and annihilated the cavalry of Lieutenant Colonel **George Armstrong Custer** at the **Battle of the Little Bighorn**. The battle left a deep and lasting mark on how Americans perceived the Native Americans and their struggle for freedom.

He went on a daring war-party raid against the **Arapaho Indians** in 1858 and was given the warrior name of Tashunca-Uitco, meaning "Crazy Horse." In 1865, he became a "shirt wearer" or protector of his people, and he participated in most of the major battles between the U.S. Army and the Indians during **Red Cloud's War** (1865–1868).

In 1876, Crazy Horse became the supreme chief of the Oglala Sioux. The U.S. War Department had ordered all Native Americans to return to their reservation lands by January 1, 1876. Disregarding this order, Crazy Horse and his fellow Sioux leader, Chief **Sitting Bull** (see no. 46), set in motion the chain of events that led to the **Great Sioux War** of 1876–1877.

On June 25, Crazy Horse and Sitting Bull led their warriors in the thrilling victory over "Yellow Hair" Custer. Despite the victory, both chiefs began moving north and west in order to avoid the retaliation they knew would come from the U.S. Army. Crazy Horse and his people were pursued relentlessly by Colonel **Nelson A. Miles**, who attacked them successfully in January 1877 at their winter camp in the Wolf Mountains. On May 6, 1877, Crazy Horse appeared at the Red Cloud Agency's Camp Robinson and surrendered along with 1,100 of his people and 2,500 ponies.

Crazy Horse

Crazy Horse spent a restless four months in relative confinement on the reservation. His questing warrior spirit did not take to living quietly, and he left the reservation without permission. On September 6, 1877, he was arrested by a large number of U.S. agents and army soldiers. When he learned that he was to be put in solitary confinement in a prison, Crazy Horse drew a knife and fought with his captors. He died in the struggle from a wound to the abdomen.

His parents buried him in an unknown location in the valley of Wounded Knee Creek. In 1947, Polish sculptor Korczak Ziolkowski, began carving a 563-foot-high statue of the chief 22 miles from Mount Rushmore, South Dakota. The sculptor's death in 1982 did not halt the work; many of his 10 children continued to labor to create a fitting monument to Crazy Horse.

54. Thomas A. Edison
(1847–1931)

The "Wizard of Menlo Park," **Thomas Alva Edison**, was born in Milan, Ohio, the youngest of seven children. His father moved the family to Port Huron, Michigan in 1854, and Edison grew up in an idyllic country environment. After being taught at home by his mother, Edison sold newspapers on the Grand Trunk Railway in Michigan at the age of 12. Both inventive and ambitious, he bought a printing press at 15 and began a small newspaper, the *Grand Trunk Herald*, which he sold between railroad stops.

Edison became a telegraph operator in 1863 and spent the next four years roaming the midwest, taking jobs here and there. He filed for his first patent in 1868 for a vote-recording machine. He received the patent in 1869 but found no buyer. Edison then formulated a basic rule he would always follow: not to invent anything without having a commercial prospect.

Moving to New York City in 1869, Edison worked for **Laws' Gold Indicator Company**. He earned $40,000 by selling the rights to a stock-ticker invention (useful on Wall Street) and established his own workshop in Newark, New Jersey. There he formed the first true U.S. research laboratory — a team of scientific workers who aimed to invent, patent and produce strictly for profit. Edison patented the diplex telegraph in 1873 and moved his workshop to Menlo Park, New Jersey, in 1876.

Edison's two most important inventions were the phonograph (1877) and the commercially practicable incandescent lamp (1879). His success with the phonograph led to the nickname "Wizard of Menlo Park," and Edison became an important celebrity. An astute businessman as well as an inventor, Edison opened the first commercial electric-light station on Pearl Street in New York City in 1882. He organized a number of companies, most notably the **Edison General Electric Company** (1889), which merged with its largest rival to form the **General Electric Company** in 1892.

Edison moved his workplace to West Orange, New Jersey in 1887. He experimented with motion pictures toward the end of the century and pioneered work in talking pictures around 1912.

Edison was president of the Naval Consulting Board during World War I, and he experimented with the development of torpedo mechanisms and submarine periscopes. A trial-and-error inventor, he came to singly or jointly hold a total of 1,093 patents, including 389 for electric light and power, 195 for the phonograph, 150 for the telegraph, 141 for storage batteries and 34 for the telephone.

Thomas A. Edison

55. Samuel Gompers
(1850–1924)

Labor leader **Samuel Gompers** was born in London, England, one of nine children of Dutch-Jewish immigrants. He left school at age 10 to work as a cigar maker. His parents brought the family to New York City in 1863, and Gompers joined Local 15 of the Cigar Makers International Union in 1864.

In his early union days, Gompers was a Marxist; he believed in the economic theories developed by the German historian and author Karl Marx in his book, *The Communist Manifesto* (1848).

Gompers changed his views, however, and by the 1870s he advocated a "pure and simple" trade unionism whereby there would be only one union for each trade or industry in all of North America. Gompers also steered away from political unionism, seeking to isolate the areas, suvh as wages and working hours, where unions could have the most effect and to leave political matters to politicians. Given this philosophy, he was much more acceptable to the American public than the more radical union men of his day. Gompers was elected vice president of the Cigar Makers International Union in 1886.

In the same year, he founded and became the first president of the **American Federation of Labor** (AFL). He was re-elected to the presidency in every year except 1895 for the rest of his life; in this capacity, Gompers became the single most influential union leader of his time. Continuing his moderate stance, he insisted unions bargain directly with employers and refrain from what he considered unnecessary political activities.

Gompers hailed Congress's passage of the **Clayton Antitrust Act** (1914) as the *Magna Carta* of the labor movement, mistakenly believing it would put an end to federal injunctions in labor disputes. When the United States entered **World War I** in 1917, he vigorously marshaled labor support and

Samuel Gompers

organized a **War Committee on Labor** to demonstrate the patriotism of the AFL. By this time, he had become the living symbol of American trade unionism. He served as a member of the **Advisory Committee to the Council of National Defense** (1917–1918) and was a member of the U.S. delegation to the **Paris Peace Conference** in 1919.

Despite his standing and clout, Gompers was unable to stem the tide that went against unions in the early 1920s. A great strike in Seattle, Washington was crushed by police, and Gompers must have been dismayed by the way the unions were often defeated by a combination of political power and strong-arm use of the police or military.

Gompers' early success had come from his moderation and willingness to work within the system as it existed. The union movement, however, would turn to much more radical measures after his death and win greater concessions from employers than had been possible during Gompers's lifetime.

56. Booker T. Washington
(1856–1915)

Born a slave on the James Burroughs plantation close to Roanoke, Virginia, **Booker Taliaferro Washington** became a visible symbol of what African-Americans could achieve in the 19th century through determination and hard work. The son of Jane Ferguson (a plantation cook) and an unknown white father, Washington grew up amid the tumult of the **Civil War**. Gaining his freedom in 1865, he moved to Malden, West Virginia.

Washington studied at Hampton Institute and Industrial School from 1872 to 1875. There he was befriended by the school's founder, General **Samuel C. Armstrong**, a missionary's son who had commanded African-American troops during the Civil War. Armstrong's belief in industrial and vocational education for African-Americans had a profound effect on his pupil and friend. Washington returned to Malden, taught school for two years, and then joined Armstrong's staff at Hampton Institute.

In 1881, Armstrong selected Washington to found a teachers' school at Tuskegee, Alabama. Washington began the **Tuskegee Normal and Industrial Institute** with a staff of three teachers and 37 students, housed in shacks. Tuskegee became the focus of Washington's life. During his long tenure as principal (1881–1915), the school grew to include a student body of 1,500 and a faculty of 180. The school became one of the leading centers of black education in the world.

Washington delivered an important address at the **Cotton States and International Exposition** in Atlanta, Georgia on September 18, 1895. He urged his fellow African-Americans, "Cast down your bucket where you are." By this he meant they should first seek to improve their economic and moral status before seeking full equality with white Americans of European descent. Regarding the matter of racial segregation, Washington declared, "In all things that are purely social we [meaning all Americans] can be as separate as the fingers, yet one as the hand in all things essential to moral progress."

The speech conferred great status on Washington, who inherited the mantle of African-American leadership from **Frederick Douglass** (see no. 39). Washington, influenced by Armstrong and his years at Hampton and Tuskegee, called for industrial and vocational education for the masses.

Washington founded, and was first president of, the **National Negro Business League**. Toward the end of his life he began to speak out more strongly against segregation. Washington's autobiography was published in three volumes: *The Story of My Life and Work* (1909), *Up From Slavery* (1910), and *My Larger Education* (1911).

Booker T. Washington

Woodrow Wilson
(1856–1924)

More truly a scholar than a politician, **Thomas Woodrow Wilson** made a profound, although complex, mark on American politics. His earliest years were spent in Augusta, Georgia throughout the **Civil War** era.

Wilson first attended Davidson College and graduated from the College of New Jersey (later Princeton University). He studied for and received his Ph.D. in history from Johns Hopkins University in 1886.

Wilson taught history and government at Bryn Mawr College (1885–1888) and Wesleyan University (1888–1890) before he went to teach at Princeton. He steadily gained a reputation with his fellow faculty, and in 1902, was elected president of the university.

In 1910, he was elected governor of New Jersey. Following the progressive politics of the Democratic Party, Wilson made New Jersey into one of the most reform-conscious states in the Union. In 1912, he won the Democratic nomination for president. The scholar-administrator then won the presidency in a year when the support of the Republican Party was divided between incumbent President **William Howard Taft** and the Bull Moose Party of **Theodore Roosevelt**.

Wilson's progressive platform brought about the creation of the **Federal Reserve System** (to regulate banking and Wall Street) and the nation's first **graduated income tax**. Wilson won re-election in 1916 with the slogan "He Kept Us Out of War," in reference to **World War I,** which had begun in Europe in 1914.

Wilson sincerely wanted to remain at peace, but the sinking of the *Lusitania* and other passenger liners with Americans aboard, combined with the German use of submarine warfare against American merchant ships, compelled him to take a dramatic step. On April 2, 1917, he appeared before Congress and asked for a declaration of war to make

Woodrow Wilson

the world "safe for Democracy." Congress voted the declaration and Wilson presided over the greatest American military buildup and effort to that date. He delivered his most important speech on January 18, 1918, calling for his plan of "**Fourteen Points**" to be used as the basis for a future peace treaty. Respect for national self-determination was the central theme of his plan.

Following the Allied victories of 1918, and the Armistice of November 11, 1918, Wilson went to Paris to lead the American peace delegation in person. He was received rapturously by enormous crowds in Paris. However, he failed to win many of his points and was outmaneuvered in the closed-door negotiations by French premier **Georges Clemenceau** and British prime minister **David Lloyd George**.

Nevertheless, Wilson returned home and campaigned vigorously but unsuccessfully for Congressional approval of the Treaty of Versailles, which included his plan for a **League of Nations** to prevent future wars. Wilson won the Nobel Peace Prize in 1920.

Theodore Roosevelt was born in New York City. An enormously inquisitive and enthusiastic youth, he was weakened early on by asthma, but he trained with weights and endurance tests to build up his strength. He graduated from Harvard in 1880. Roosevelt practiced law, but felt more drawn to politics. His first elected office was that of New York State assemblyman (1882–1884).

Roosevelt served on the Civil Service Commission from 1889 to 1895 and as president of the Board of Police Commissioners for New York City from 1895 to 1897. His vigorous campaigning for the successful election of **William McKinley** as president in 1896 brought him the appointment as assistant secretary of the Navy (1897–1898).

Roosevelt resigned from the Navy in 1898 to command a regiment called the "**Rough Riders**," in the crucial **Battle of San Juan Hill** during the **Spanish-American War**. Returning home after the war, he was elected governor of New York in 1899 and served in that post until he was elected vice president under McKinley in 1900. Upon McKinley's assassination in September 1901, Roosevelt became the youngest person ever to assume the presidency of the United States.

Roosevelt clearly relished the role of chief executive. Believing in progressive politics, he "busted" a number of financial trusts and gave assistance to labor unions during his time in office.

In foreign affairs, he believed in carrying a "big stick," something he demonstrated numerous times, especially in Pan-American relations. He announced the "**Roosevelt Corollary**" to the **Monroe Doctrine** to assert that the United States might act as a police force in regard to maintaining peace among its Central American neighbors.

In 1903, Roosevelt began negotiations with the South American nation of Colombia, seeking to purchase a narrow strip of land through which a canal might be dug. Encountering obstacles in the negotiations, he promptly supported a revolution in the northern part of Colombia that led to the formation of the Republic of Panama. Roosevelt then obtained a treaty for the construction of the 50-mile **Panama Canal**, which thereby gave the United States a much faster route between the Atlantic and Pacific oceans. Roosevelt also sent the "**Great White Fleet**" of American battleships around the world (1906–1907) to impress foreigners with the young nation's naval power.

Roosevelt left office in 1909, after two terms.

Dissatisfied with the policies of his successor, **William Howard Taft**, Roosevelt ran again for president in 1912, but his creation of a splinter Republican group, known as the **Bull Moose Party**, ensured the Democratic ticket headed by **Woodrow Wilson** (see no. 57) would win that year.

Theodore Roosevelt

One of the greatest American philosophers and educators, **John Dewey** believed that direct experience was the surest route to knowledge and wisdom. His analytical and pragmatic approach to intellectual matters rendered him the single most important spokesperson for American education for more than 40 years.

Born in Burlington, Vermont, Dewey was the son of Vermont farmers. His father was a grocer, a quartermaster (in charge of the soldiers' food) during the **Civil War**, and then a tobacco-seller. Dewey graduated from the University of Vermont (1879) and went to Johns Hopkins University to study psychology. His doctoral thesis, *The Psychology of Kant*, marked him as a rising academic talent, and he went to teach at the University of Michigan in 1889.

Dewey began his long list of important publications with *Psychology*, published in 1887. He proceeded to write *The School and Society* (1899), *How We Think* (1910), *Schools of To-Morrow* (1915) and *Democracy and Education* (1916).

In these and many other publications, he came to espouse four core beliefs that have had a profound influence on American education in the 20th century. First, he believed in "**radical empiricism**," meaning that one must trust one's experience — things actually are as they are experienced. Second, Dewey believed in "**instrumentalism**," ideas are essentially plans of action and that they arise in response to specific problems. Third, he espoused the cause of "**experimentalism**," ideas must always be subjected to experiment. Fourth, he announced his belief in "**pragmatism**," that an idea must be judged by whether it works in practice.

Some critics have asserted that Dewey imparted a dry and lifeless quality to American thought and education, others have

John Dewey

applauded his ideas and declared that he was, after **Ralph Waldo Emerson** (see no. 32), the most profound and independent-minded thinker in American history.

Dewey left Michigan to teach philosophy and pedagogy at the University of Chicago (1894–1904) and then philosophy at Columbia University (1905–1930). Sometimes contradictory in his beliefs, he supported progressive and Socialist candidates at the start of the century, then opposed the reforms of **Franklin D. Roosevelt**'s **New Deal** during the 1930s (see no. 70). He made visits to Japan, China and the Soviet Union, and his thoughts on international affairs and other matters of concern were given great weight by American newspapers.

Dewey died in New York City, leaving behind a remarkable career with many honors and laurels bestowed upon him. Many Americans continue to believe that the essentially American characteristics of pragmatic action were expressed in ideas by America's greatest philosopher.

60. William Jennings Bryan
(1860–1925)

The voice of the farmers of the Great Plains states and the midwest, **William Jennings Bryan** was perhaps the single most notable orator the United States ever produced. Born in Salem, Illinois, he graduated from Illinois College and Union College of Law in Chicago.

Bryan served in the U.S. House of Representatives (1891–1895), where he became recognized as a spokesperson for farmers and the free coinage of silver at a fixed rate with that of gold. He ran for the U.S. Senate in 1894, but lost the election.

He spent a year in journalism and lecturing and then went as a delegate to the Democratic National Convention in 1896. There he delivered the greatest speech of his life and, some would say, the greatest of all American political speeches. Arguing for the interests of the embattled farmers against the moneyed interests of the east coast, his "Cross of Gold" speech became the central part of the Democratic platform, and Bryan was nominated to run for president although he was only 36 years old!

Running against Republican **William McKinley** (1843–1901), Bryan campaigned in 27 states and made more than 600 speeches. He won most of the southern states and those west of the Mississippi River, but lost the general election to McKinley. Undaunted, Bryan ran against McKinley in 1900, this time arguing against American annexation of the Philippine Islands which had been taken from Spain in the **Spanish-American War**. Bryan lost again. Although he would run one more losing race (against Republican **William Howard Taft** in 1908), he never polled better numbers than in his original bid for the office in 1896.

Bryan founded a publication, *The Commoner*, in 1901 and continued his propaganda campaign against the moneyed classes of the nation. His help was instrumental in **Woodrow Wilson**'s 1912 presidential victory (see no. 57). Wilson rewarded Bryan with the post of Secretary of State. Bryan excelled in this role. He negotiated a total of 30 treaties in two years, all but two of which were approved by the U.S. Senate.

Bryan moved to Miami, Florida in 1920 and made a fortune in the booming real estate market there. His last public appearance came in 1925 when he spoke for the prosecution in the Scopes "Monkey Trial" in Tennessee; John T. Scopes was accused of teaching evolution theory rather than Christian doctrine in public schools. Bryan's efforts prevailed and the prosecution won the day, but he had been embarrassed by the more eloquent and up-to-date language of defense lawyer **Clarence Darrow**.

Bryan belongs in a small class of noted American orators — along with **Daniel Webster** (see no. 22), **Henry Clay** (see no. 20) and **John C. Calhoun** (see no. 23) — men who voiced important issues and tried, but failed, to obtain the highest office of the land.

William Jennings Bryan

Henry Ford

The maker of the famed Model T and Model A automobiles, **Henry Ford** was born in Greenfield, Michigan to Irish-American parents. He attended school until the age of 15, when he became a machinist's apprentice in Detroit. Starting from these modest beginnings, Ford began to experiment with engines in 1890, and by 1896, he had built his first automobile (which is still on display in the Greenfield Village Museum).

In 1888, he married Clara Bryant of Michigan. The couple had one child named Edsel Bryant Ford.

Ford left his secure position as chief engineer of the Edison Company in Detroit to organize the **Detroit Auto Company** (1899).

In 1903, he solicited financial partners who joined him to launch the **Ford Motor Company** with an original capitalization of $100,000.

The true start to Ford's remarkable success came in 1908 with the appearance of the all-black **Model T** car, intended for the public at large. Ford brought engineers and machines to his plant in suburban Highland Park that specialized in the mechanics of "mass production," and by 1913 he was able to sell the Model T for just $500. The following year he announced his intent to pay all his auto workers a minimum wage of $5 a day, which was at least 15 percent higher than the wages paid by any of his competitors. At the same time, he staunchly resisted any attempts to unionize his workers and was quick to bring in company police to stifle any hint of organized labor.

He ran for the U.S. Senate in 1918; upon losing the election he blamed Jews and international bankers for his defeat (Ford harbored an extreme distrust of banks, and he was clearly anti-Semitic). In 1919, he bought out all the remaining stockholders in the Ford Motor Company and from that point on, ran the auto giant to suit himself. The Ford family retained complete control from 1919 to 1956.

Ford did not move with the times, and his company fell behind in the field of auto innovation. His new **Model A**, brought out in 1927, was a hit with the public, but he resisted innovations such as the conventional gearshift, hydraulic brakes, and six- and eight-cylinder engines.

After the U.S. entered World War II, Ford established a plant at Willow Run, Michigan that produced numerous B-24 bombers for the American war effort. Ford turned over control of the company to his son Edsel, whose early death yielded power to Ford's grandson, **Henry Ford II**.

The son of a prominent newspaper owner and philanthropic mother, **William Randolph Hearst** was born in San Francisco, California. He attended Harvard and was business manager of the *Lampoon* (a student magazine), but he was expelled for pranks he played on one of his professors. He left Harvard with no degree and was given control of the *San Francisco Examiner* by his father in 1887. Hearst took over what had been an ailing newspaper and soon turned it into a thriving concern. He used a combination of sensational news reporting and the promotion of a civic reform program to excite the reading public. This early success led to his purchase of the *New York Morning Journal* in 1895.

Hearst went to New York and entered into a great circulation contest with **Joseph Pulitzer**, who owned the *New York World*. The rivals constantly raised the stakes in their struggle to outsell each other.

Many historians believe their sensational reporting of the rebellion in Spanish Cuba and the explosion of the U.S. battleship *Maine* in 1898 directly led to the **Spanish-American War**. Both Pulitzer and Hearst were accused of "**yellow journalism**," inciting people to activity through exaggerated news reporting (the term came from an early comic strip known as the *Yellow Kid*).

Hearst thrived on the circulation battle and went on to acquire or develop newspapers in Chicago (1902), Boston and Los Angeles (1904). He founded the **International News Service** in 1909 and built an enormous market for popular magazines such as *Cosmopolitan, Good Housekeeping, Town and Country and Harper's Bazaar.*

Hearst's remarkable success came from his pioneering efforts in the journalism field. He introduced aspects of newspapers that all Americans now take for granted: color

William Randolph Hearst

comics, Sunday supplements, banner headlines and editorial crusading. By 1937, he controlled an immense communications empire that included 25 large daily newspapers as well as radio stations and motion picture interests.

Hearst was frustrated, however, in his attempts to win high political office. He did serve as a New York congressman in the U.S. House of Representatives (1903–1907), but his races for the U.S. Senate, governor of New York and mayor of New York City, all ended in defeat.

Weary of East Coast politics, he moved to California's central coast in 1927 where he built the largest estate in North America at the time, **San Simeon**. His property spanned 240,000 acres, had 50 miles of ocean frontage on the Pacific, and contained four castles in which were housed many notable works of art. During the **Great Depression** (1929–1940), he was forced to sell some of his valuable paintings. He became a recluse in his later years, spending most of his time alone on the San Simeon estate.

The sons of a minister, brothers **Wilbur** and **Orville Wright** grew up in Dayton, Ohio. From an early age, they showed a profound interest in mechanical matters.

They went into business together, renting and selling bicycles, but in time they began to design and make them; they built the Van Cleve bicycle together. Apparently carefree and lighthearted, the brothers found their true mission in 1896, when they heard about the death of German glider expert Otto Lilienthal. They read all they could find on the subject of flying and learned much more by studying the flights of birds. They gleaned an understanding of how birds twist their wings in order to control their movements.

The brothers experimented with their first driveable glider at **Kitty Hawk**, North Carolina in 1900. They returned the next year and also practiced the mechanics of flight by making a six-foot wind tunnel in their shop in Ohio. By 1903, the brothers had made reliable mathematical tables on the effect of air pressure on curved surfaces.

They brought their third glider (powered by a four-cylinder engine) to North Carolina and, on December 17, 1903, Orville made the first known air flight, traveling 120 feet in 12 seconds in the air. They made three more flights in "**Flyer I**" that day, the longest being 852 feet during 59 seconds in the air with Wilbur as the pilot. Five witnesses testified to the flights.

The Wright brothers proceeded to experiment at Huffman Prairie near Dayton, with "**Flyer II**" (1904) and "**Flyer III**" (1905).

Unable at first to attract a buyer or the interest of the U.S. government, the brothers chose not to fly at all between October 1905 and May 1908. In 1908, Wilbur went to France and undertook spectacular demonstrations of flight to admiring crowds at Le Mans, while Orville did the same at Fort Myer,

Wilbur and Orville Wright

Virginia. Orville survived a crash that killed one of his passengers, and he continued to fly.

By 1909, the brothers had closed a contract with a German firm as well as attracting the interest of the U.S. military. They formed the **Wright Company** in New York City, but had to devote much of their time in costly lawsuits to protect their invention from imitators.

Wilbur died of typhoid fever in 1912. Orville sold his interest in the Wright Company and retired to pursue his research interests in private. He received the first Daniel Guggenheim Medal in 1929. Posthumously, Wilbur and Orville Wright were named to the American Hall of Fame in 1955.

64. Frank Lloyd Wright
(1867–1959)

Frank Lloyd Wright endured numerous personal and financial difficulties during his long life to emerge triumphant as the most acclaimed American architect of the 20th century. Wright developed a great love of the land and respect for organic forms. He would later be the spokesperson for organic architecture that "develops from within, outward."

Wright studied civil engineering at the University of Wisconsin. He moved to Chicago, where he learned architecture in the office of **Louis Henri Sullivan** (1856–1924).

Wright set up his own practice in 1893, and the first phase of his career (1893–1911) made him the leader of the new "prairie" school of architecture, one that emphasized long, horizontal buildings with few walls between the living spaces.

His personal life, however, was deeply troubled. He married Catherine Tobin in 1889, but in 1904 he became entranced by Mamah Borthwick Cheney, for whom he was designing a house. He and Cheney each asked their spouses for divorces. Mrs. Wright refused, and Frank Lloyd Wright went to Germany for two years (1909–1911).

During this time, he and Cheney lived as a married couple. They returned to the U.S. in 1911, and lived at **Taliesin** (a Welsh word meaning "shining brow"). Mrs. Cheney and four of her children by her marriage (to Mr. Cheney) were killed by an insane servant at Taliesin in 1913. Wright then went to Japan (1916–1921), where he designed the **Imperial Hotel** in Tokyo, which withstood the great Kanto earthquake of 1923 one year after it was completed.

Always more interested in his artistic work than in practical details, Wright fell into serious financial trouble and a bank took Taliesin away from him. He was rescued only when a group of friends and admirers formed Wright, Incorporated, which sheltered him from creditors and allowed him to continue his architecture in peace.

Few commissions were given during the height of the **Great Depression**, but in 1936, Wright commenced the third, final and most victorious phase of his career. He designed **Fallingwater** in the Allegheny mountains near Pittsburgh, Pennsylvania. Probably his most popular work, it attracted millions of visitors. He went on to design and build **Taliesin West** in Scottsdale, Arizona and the **Guggenheim Museum** in New York City. Wright received the **American Institute of Architects**' gold medal in 1949.

Wright was commissioned to design the master plan for the Marin County (California) civic center in 1957 at the age of 90. He died before ground was broken in 1960, but he completed the major design work, highlighted by two four-story wings merged beneath an 80-foot-diameter dome capping the county library and accented by a slim gold tower.

Frank Lloyd Wright

Through the twists and turns of a remarkable life and career, **William Edward Burghardt Du Bois** became perhaps the single most influential African-American leader of the 20th century. Born in Great Barrington, Massachusetts, he was encouraged by the Congregational church there to further his studies. He went south and graduated from Fisk University in Nashville, Tennessee (1888) and was shocked by the level of racial hatred and segregation he encountered in the region. He went to Harvard and earned his Ph.D. in history (1895) after studying in Germany at the University of Berlin for two years.

Du Bois went to Philadelphia, Pennsylvania and conducted the first-ever case study of an African-American community; the result was his book *The Philadelphia Negro* (1899). He received an appointment to teach history and sociology at Atlanta University in 1898 and remained there for 12 years, during which time he published a number of monographs on sociological topics.

In the first decade of the 20th century, he clashed vigorously with **Booker T. Washington** (see no. 56), who believed African-Americans should work their way up the economic ladder through vocational training rather than through academic advancement. Du Bois founded the **Niagara Movement**, which dedicated itself to the overall advancement of African-Americans, and he published his best-known work, *The Souls of Black Folk*.

W. E. B. Du Bois

In 1910, he became editor of the magazine *Crisis: A Record of the Darker Races* (1910–1934) for the new **National Association for the Advancement of Colored People** (NAACP). Du Bois served faithfully until the **Great Depression** of the 1930s, when he urged African-Americans to create a separate "group economy" from white Americans. He resigned from the NAACP, asserting that the group advanced the interests only of the black middle class, not the oppressed black workers.

Du Bois wrote a masterly autobiography, *Dusk of Dawn: An Essay Toward an Autobiography of a Race Concept* (1940). At the age of 73, he returned to the NAACP and worked in a research position (1944–1948) until he left the organization after a bitter quarrel over how African-American aspirations should be attained.

In 1951, Du Bois was accused by the U.S. government of being an unregistered agent of a foreign power (the Soviet Union), and his passport was revoked. The humiliation of being labeled an agent turned him thoroughly away from support of mainstream American values. He became a member of the Communist Party at age 93 in 1961. That same year, he moved to Ghana, Africa. He renounced his United States citizenship in 1962 and died in Ghana on August 27, 1963, exactly one day prior to the enormous and influential "**March on Washington**," led by the Reverend **Martin Luther King, Jr.** (see no. 96).

66. Margaret Sanger
(1879–1966)

Social reformer **Margaret Sanger** was born Margaret Louise Higgins in Corning, New York. She graduated from Claverack College in the Catskills (1899) and studied nursing at White Plains Hospital and the Manhattan Eye and Ear Hospital. In 1902, she married architect William Sanger.

The family moved to New York City in 1912, and Margaret soon found herself engaged in the stimulating intellectual ferment that surrounded her there. Friendly with Emma Goldman, Alexander Berkman and other radicals, Sanger became firmly convinced of the necessity of birth control for women following the death (in her arms) of a 28-year-old mother from the city's tenements.

Margaret Sanger

Sanger founded *The Woman Rebel* (1914), a monthly magazine, and soon coined the term "**birth control**." Her efforts to educate the public led to continual trouble with the law; she was indicted in 1915 for sending information on birth control through the mail. Her action had violated the "**Comstock Law**," passed in 1873.

On October 16, 1916, Sanger and a number of associates opened the first birth control clinic in the United States in the Brownsville section of Brooklyn. Nine days later the clinic was raided by police and Sanger was arrested and jailed for her defiance of New York laws, which forbade even giving advice about contraception.

At her trial in early 1917, Sanger refused to repent for her actions, declaring that "I cannot promise to obey a law I do not respect." She was found guilty and confined to a New York workhouse for 30 days. This brief jail sentence led to greater publicity and even some fame for Sanger. She founded the **National Birth Control League**, which would later become the **Planned Parenthood Federation of America**.

Sanger went on a worldwide speaking tour in 1922 to bring further attention to her cause. Most of her speeches began with the words, "The first right of every child is to be wanted, to be desired, to be planned with an intensity of love that gives it its title to being."

She tried unsuccessfully to have the "Doctor's Bill" passed by Congress. The bill failed for the last time in 1934, but Sanger and her allies prevailed in a U.S. circuit court ruling *United States v. One Package* (1936). Judge Grover Moscowitz ruled that a new model of Japanese diaphragm (which had been sent to Sanger but was confiscated by the Post Office) must be delivered. From that time on, American women had the unimpeded right that Sanger had sought for them — to legally obtain birth control.

Born near Lucas, Iowa, **John Llewellyn Lewis** was the oldest son of Welsh immigrants. He left school at the age of 15 to work in the local coal mines. In 1901, he became secretary of the local chapter of the **United Mine Workers of America** (UMWA).

In the coal mines, Lewis entered an industry that was the lifeblood of the American economy. Coal was king at the start of the 20th century. Mining workers obtained little of the profits; many workers became ill, disabled, or were killed outright as they worked. Therefore, Lewis and others like him tried to make the UMWA strong, so as to gain safer working conditions.

Lewis became an organizer for the **American Federation of Labor** (AFL) in 1911. He was seldom at home during the next six years as he traveled the country, seeking to bring more workers into the AFL. In 1919, he was named acting president of the 400,000-member UMWA. He immediately led the coal workers on a national strike and was rewarded by the membership with his election to the union presidency a year later.

The 1920s was a painful decade for Lewis and the union; membership dropped from 400,000 to less than 150,000. The onset of the **Great Depression** brought about an increase in membership, and in strikes. Lewis formed the **Congress of Industrial Organizations** (CIO) in 1935. The new union reflected his belief in industrial unionism and represented a complete break with trade unionism.

Lewis led the coal miners on strikes during the Great Depression and **World War II**. Originally a great hero for the leftist cause in America, Lewis later was castigated for taking the miners out on strike during the war, when such an action could endanger the war effort of the entire nation.

Lewis also made a political blunder; he

John L. Lewis

alienated **Franklin D. Roosevelt** (see no. 70). Lewis supported FDR for election in 1932 and 1936, but in 1940, Lewis changed his ideas and vowed he would resign as president of the CIO if Roosevelt were elected for a third term. FDR won the election, and Lewis stepped down. However, he remained head of the UMWA.

Lewis won many victories. Because of his work, the UMWA workers obtained both higher wages and better working conditions. Lewis was also the embodiment of aggressive unionism to the entire country. He stood for the working person's determination to obtain a fair deal in the marketplace.

68. George C. Marshall, Jr.
(1880–1959)

One of the most distinguished and dignified of all American public servants, **George C. Marshall, Jr.**, came from a well-to-do family in Uniontown, Pennsylvania. He graduated from Virginia Military Institute in 1901, was commissioned in the army in 1902, and served during the insurrection in the Philippines (1902–1903).

Marshall was one of the first American officers to take ship for France when the U.S. entered **World War I** in 1917. He was appointed chief of operations of the First Division and then the First Army. He distinguished himself through brilliant staff work and coordination that enabled 400,000 French and Italian troops to exit an area while 700,000 U.S. troops entered it. The ensuing Meuse-Argonne campaign probably could not have been conducted or won without Marshall's organizing abilities.

Marshall served in China from 1924 to 1927 and organized the **Civilian Conservation Corps** when the **New Deal** began in 1933. He was chief of the army's war plans division from 1938 to 1939, and when **World War II** started, he was made chief of staff of the U.S. Army. Marshall yearned to be more actively involved in the war; he wanted desperately to lead the American invasion of France on D-Day, but President **Franklin D. Roosevelt** (see no. 70) told him that his talents were needed in Washington, D.C. to coordinate the war effort. Marshall continued to work his magic on the endless stream of details that came from organizing an army of 12 million soldiers. Marshall achieved the rank of general of the army in 1944.

After the war ended, Marshall served on a peace mission to China in 1946 and then was named Secretary of State by President **Harry S. Truman**. In his new post, Marshall was instrumental in the creation of a plan to send capital and resources to European countries

that had been devastated by the war. The "**Marshall Plan**" was extremely important in keeping countries such as France, Italy and Greece in the democratic camp in the aftermath of the war. Again, Marshall's vision and ability to implement plans proved invaluable.

Marshall resigned as Secretary of State in 1949, citing poor health, and became president of the **American Red Cross**. With the start of the **Korean War**, he returned to government and served as Secretary of Defense from 1950 to 1951.

He retired permanently, leaving a nearly spotless record after 49 years in military and government service. One of his greatest accolades came from Secretary of War **Henry L. Stimson** who told Marshall, "I have seen a great many soldiers in my lifetime and you, sir, are the finest soldier I have ever known."

George C. Marshall, Jr.

Cecil B. DeMille

The quintessential Hollywood movie director, **Cecil B. DeMille** was born in Ashfield, Massachusetts and grew up in New York City. The son of a playwright and lay preacher, DeMille graduated from Pennsylvania Military College and then the American Academy of Dramatic Arts in New York City (1900). He made his Broadway acting debut in *Hearts Are Trumps* (1900).

In 1914, DeMille made one of the first feature-length films shot in **Hollywood**, California. *The Squaw Man* was about an Englishman who marries a Native American. DeMille had intended to shoot the film in Flagstaff, Arizona but finding he disliked the weather, he moved the cast to Hollywood.

DeMille's decision paved the way for thousands of films in the future to be shot in southern California.

DeMille made some 20 films during **World War I**, nearly all of which focused on patriotic themes. Sensing a turn in the public mood after the war ended, he proceeded to make risqué comedies such as *Male and Female* (1919) and *Adam's Rib* (1923). DeMille was the first director to make films that used bathroom and bedroom scenes, and by the mid-1920s his career seemed doomed to be limited to comedies about sex.

Once again DeMille gauged the public mood and found that Americans wanted still more sex and glamour in their movies — but sex with a point or moral. Therefore, he became the master of the religious epic, couching sexual and melodramatic themes within such films as *The Ten Commandments* (1923) and *The King of Kings* (1927). Strutting about the film set in a wide-brimmed hat, an open-neck shirt and riding breeches, DeMille became an icon of his genre, and some people began to call him "The Greatest Filmmaker on Earth."

In his later years, DeMille amplified the skills he had already shown, rather than attempting to develop new ones. He made epic western movies such as *Union Pacific* (1939). He made his only brief screen appearance in *Sunset Boulevard* (1950). In 1956, he issued the monumental remake of *The Ten Commandments* starring **Charlton Heston**, **Yul Brynner** and **Edward G. Robinson**.

More original in the art of filmmaking than in screenwriting, he pioneered lighting effects and the use of color film. He produced and directed nearly 70 films, most of which were quite unmemorable to sophisticated audiences, but thrilled many Americans looking for entertainment and diversion from their everyday lives.

70. Franklin D. Roosevelt
(1882–1945)

No American political leader has exerted as much direct, personal influence on American history as did **Franklin Delano Roosevelt**, the only person ever to be elected to four terms as president of the United States.

In 1913, President **Woodrow Wilson** appointed Roosevelt assistant Secretary of the Navy. He thrived in this capacity, and in 1920, considered himself ready for an attempt at higher office.

Roosevelt was stricken with polio in 1921. Before long, the ebullient and expansive politician could not stand or move his legs. However, he took a decisive position for his future. For the first time confronted by something that could overwhelm him, Roosevelt chose to confront the illness head-on. He overcame his disability through vigorous exercises in water and through the use of a wheelchair, and was always supported by the arms of political aides in public.

Roosevelt returned to politics in 1924 and was elected governor of New York in 1928. Success followed success, and in 1932, he won the presidential election over incumbent **Herbert Hoover**, who had been discredited by the **Great Depression**, which began in 1929 during his term.

From the start, Roosevelt was vigorous and optimistic. He pumped millions of dollars into the economy and pushed Congress to pass the **Agricultural Adjustment Act**, establish the **Civilian Conservation Corps** and pass the **National Industrial Recovery Act.** Roosevelt energized the nation with constant, relentless enthusiasm during his weekly "fireside chats" on the radio.

Roosevelt foresaw the dangers posed by Nazi dictator **Adolf Hitler** and Italian fascist **Benito Mussolini** before many of his policymakers did. Almost immediately after **World War II** began (1939), Roosevelt wanted to enter the war. Unfortunately, the spirit of

"**Isolationism**" in American society prevented any such action until the Japanese — who had not consulted with either their German or Italian allies — chose to attack and bomb the American fleet at **Pearl Harbor** near Honolulu, Hawaii on December 7, 1941. Dramatically calling the attack "a day that will live in infamy," Roosevelt called for and received a declaration of war.

Roosevelt was truly the military commander-in-chief throughout the war, and directed the actions and policies of the war effort. Charming to the public, dominant with his Cabinet and ferocious toward the dictators, Roosevelt exerted a stronger presence in international affairs than any other American, before or since.

By early 1945, it was apparent that the United States and Allies would win the war; it was also apparent that Roosevelt was weakening physically. He died on April 12, leaving behind a stunned nation that was first in the world in military strength, economic influence and national spirit.

Franklin D. Roosevelt

Eleanor Roosevelt
(1884–1962)

Eleanor Roosevelt was born in New York City, the oldest child of Elliott and Anna Roosevelt. She attended a girls' school where the headmistress, Marie Souvestre, took her under her wing. The three happiest years of Eleanor's girlhood were spent at the school.

In 1905, she married **Franklin Delano Roosevelt** (see no. 70), her fifth cousin once removed. Eleanor found herself constantly thwarted by her matriarchal mother-in-law, Sara Roosevelt. It was not until 1910, when her husband began his political career in earnest, that Eleanor began to find outlets for her remarkable energy.

While Franklin rose from New York state assemblyman to assistant Secretary of the Navy, and then to governor of New York, Eleanor distinguished herself in Red Cross work (during World War I) and in service with the **League of Women Voters** and the **Women's Trade Union League**. From soldiers in hospitals to mothers at soup kitchens, everyday people found her a tremendous source of inspiration.

When Roosevelt became president of the United States in 1933, Eleanor became the unofficial spokesperson for millions of poor and disenfranchised Americans. She wrote *My Day*, a daily syndicated column. She traveled the country finding those Americans who had no voice in the political process due to poverty and neglect. She became the most ardent champion of a law against lynching, championed the rights of African-Americans, and resigned from the **Daughters of the American Revolution** after they refused to allow an African-American singer named **Marian Anderson** to perform in their concert hall. She formed strong bonds with young people and encouraged their participation in politics. It is no exaggeration to say that her indefatigable spirit was one of the essential pieces that held Americans together during

Eleanor Roosevelt

the misery of the **Great Depression**.

After President Roosevelt died in 1945, Eleanor assumed that her public life was over. However, President **Harry Truman** appointed her one of the American delegates to the United Nations. She was instrumental in writing the **Universal Declaration of Human Rights** (1948). Eleanor also became an outspoken advocate for the fledgling state of Israel.

Roosevelt resigned from her UN post in 1953. By this time, however, she had truly become the "first lady of the world," recognized, sought after and admired by millions of people around the globe.

She campaigned hard for her beloved friend **Adlai Stevenson** (see no. 77), who ran twice for president. She was not an early advocate of **John F. Kennedy** (see no. 92), but when he reached the presidency, he appointed her chairperson of the **Commission on the Status of Women**. She died from a rare form of tuberculosis in New York City.

72. Dwight D. Eisenhower
(1890–1969)

The man whose charming smile would have such an effect on American soldiers during World War II, and the American public in the 1950s, was born **Dwight David Eisenhower** in Denison, Texas. He graduated 61st in a class of 164 from the **U.S. Military Academy at West Point** in 1915, where he was a football star.

Eisenhower graduated from the Command and General Staff School in 1926. He served as an aide to General **Douglas MacArthur** in the Philippines from 1935 to 1939, and just prior to the start of **World War II**, he caught the eye of General **George Marshall** (see no. 68).

In 1942, he was made commanding general of American troops in the European theater and directed the American landings in North Africa, Sicily and Italy. Eisenhower was assigned as Supreme Commander of the Expeditionary Allied Force in 1944 for the projected invasion of France.

Eisenhower excelled in the grueling post of supreme commander. Few military men could have won the approval of such demanding generals as **Bernard L. Montgomery** and **George S. Patton** in the way Eisenhower did. It was he who made the crucial decision to go forward on **D-Day**, June 6, 1944, in spite of potential weather storms that could have threatened the invasion of Europe. And it was Eisenhower who directed the strategy that took the Allied forces across the Rhine River into Germany (although critics then and now assert he should have pushed on and taken Berlin before the Russians did). Eisenhower was made a five-star general.

Eisenhower returned to the United States and served first as army chief of staff (1946-1948), then as president of Columbia University (1948-1950). He then reentered government service, and he served as the Supreme Commander of the **North Atlantic Treaty Organization** (NATO) from 1950 to 1952.

When he ran for president as a Republican in 1952, "I like Ike" became a ubiquitous bumper sticker across the country, and he swept into office, ending 20 years of Democratic control of the White House.

Although Eisenhower displayed a low-key, relaxed image, he was an effective and hardworking president. He ended American participation in the **Korean War**, sent marines to Lebanon in 1958, and carried out massive counterintelligence actions that toppled Communist governments in Iran and Guatemala, all the while appearing to play the role of an easygoing grandfather to the American people.

He left the White House in 1961 with a warning to Americans of the danger of the **"military-industrial complex"**; ironically, he had contributed a great deal of energy toward building that very institution.

Dwight D. Eisenhower

73. Harry L. Hopkins
(1890–1946)

Harry Lloyd Hopkins was born in Sioux City, Iowa. Hopkins was an average student at Grinnell College (in Grinnell, Iowa), where he graduated in 1912. After a short period of indecision about his career goals, he went to New York City and joined the staff of Christadora House, a welfare center supported by private means.

Hopkins advanced rapidly in the field of social work. He managed the southern division of the **Red Cross** during **World War I** and worked for the New York Association for Improving the Conditions of the Poor. He served as director of the **New York Tuberculosis Association** from 1924 to 1929, prior to his meeting and becoming close friends with Governor **Franklin D. Roosevelt** (see no. 70) of New York. Roosevelt appointed Hopkins director of New York Temporary Emergency Relief in 1931, and in 1933, he went with FDR to Washington, D.C. as part of the new Roosevelt administration.

Hopkins became one of the most influential administrators of the **New Deal** social programs. Roosevelt named him director of the **Federal Emergency Relief Administration** (FERA). In this capacity, he distributed between $8–$10 billion worth of aid. In 1935, he became the head of the **Works Progress Administration**, which included the **National Youth Administration** and the **Emergency Educational Program**. Hopkins made the difficult transition from providing direct relief for hungry citizens to providing work relief so they could sustain themselves. He also helped to set up the new **Social Security** system, and later served as Secretary of Commerce from 1938 to 1940.

The U.S. entry into **World War II** called him to serve in a new, largely unofficial, but tremendously important capacity — personal aide to the president. Between 1941 and

A montage of Harry Hopkins

1945, Hopkins was at Roosevelt's side at every major conference held on the war. He negotiated directly with foreign leaders such as **Joseph Stalin** and **Winston Churchill** (who called him "Lord Root of the Matter"), and never lost the confidence of Roosevelt. Following Roosevelt's death, the new president, **Harry S. Truman**, sent Hopkins to Russia to assure Stalin that American policy had not changed. Hopkins retired from White House service in 1945.

He became chairperson of the Women's Cloak and Suit Industry in New York City prior to his death in 1946. Winston Churchill was quoted as saying, "A strong, bright, fierce flame has burned out a frail body. … We do well to salute his memory. We shall not see his like again."

Earl Warren
(1891–1974)

One of the most influential of all American justices, **Earl Warren** grew up in southern California and studied at the University of California at Berkeley, where he received his law degree in 1914.

Warren was the deputy district attorney of Alameda County, California from 1920 to 1925 and was the district attorney from 1925 to 1939. He then served as state attorney general from 1939 to 1943 before being elected governor of California in 1942. A liberal Republican, Warren became a very popular and successful chief executive of the state. He was re-elected by large margins in 1946 and 1950, becoming the first man to serve three terms as governor of California.

Warren's career took a new and sudden shift in 1953, when President **Dwight D. Eisenhower** (see no. 72) nominated him to be Chief Justice of the United States following the death of Chief Justice **Fred M. Vinson**. Although many people hailed the appointment, some critics pointed out that Warren, who had been a lawyer, district attorney and governor, had never served for even a day as a judge at the state or federal level.

Warren took his seat on the bench in late 1953 and was confirmed by the U.S. Senate in March 1954. Only two months later, on May 17, 1954, he read the court's unanimous decision in the case *Brown v. Board of Education* that "separate educational facilities are inherently unequal," thereby officially declaring an end to **racial segregation** in American schools.

The "Warren Court" lasted from 1953 to 1969 and proceeded to hand down a number of important decisions that directly affected the lives of millions of Americans. In *Engel v. Vitale* (1962), the Court ruled that state-sponsored prayer in public schools was unconstitutional. In *Reynolds v. Sims* (1964), the judges declared the rule of "**one man, one vote**" required that all state legislators be elected from districts that were roughly equal in population. The landmark ruling in *Miranda v. Arizona* (1966) stated that suspects being held by police for questioning had to be informed of their rights — including the right to legal counsel — and if the police failed in that duty, then any of the suspects' confessions would be invalid.

Warren lead the seven-member **Warren Commission** in 1963 and 1964, which found after a 10-month investigation, that **Lee Harvey Oswald** had acted alone in his assassination of President **John F. Kennedy** (see no. 92). Hailed at the time it was published, the report came under scrutiny and attack in subsequent years. Warren announced his intention to resign in 1968, but at the request of President **Richard M. Nixon** (see no. 89), he agreed to stay on until 1969.

Earl Warren

75. **J. Edgar Hoover**
(1895–1972)

Born in Washington, D.C., **John Edgar Hoover** was the son of a civil servant. He went to George Washington University to study law, receiving his degree in 1916. He entered the U.S. Department of Justice in 1917 and soon became special assistant to Attorney General **A. Mitchell Palmer**.

During the notorious "**Red Scare**" of 1918–1919, Hoover rounded up, investigated and deported a number of alien agitators suspected of harboring communist sympathies. Although he disliked the brutal nature of this assignment, Hoover never altered his basic opinion that Communism was a danger to the United States.

Hoover was promoted to assistant director of the Justice Department's **Bureau of Investigation** in 1921. He became acting director in 1924, and in December of that year, was confirmed as director. From that time until his death — a span of nearly 48 years — he ran the bureau, which he reorganized and renamed the **Federal Bureau of Investigation** (FBI) in 1935. Hoover established a national fingerprint file. He also set up an academy to train his agents and established a crime lab, which used state-of-the-art technology in examining evidence.

The decade of the 1930s was an unusually violent time in American society. The kidnapping of the infant son of aviator **Charles A. Lindbergh** (see no. 81) in 1932 led to a series of laws being passed against kidnapping. Congress also passed other federal laws in an attempt to stem the rising tide of bootlegging and bank robbery brought on by **Prohibition** and the **Great Depression**. Seeking to put the FBI out in front during this era, Hoover promoted the image of the "**G-men**," using movies, newsreels and even comic strips to carry the message that his detectives were invincible — and they always caught the bad guys. Hoover himself went into the field to

J. Edgar Hoover

capture notorious bank robbers like Alvin "Creepy" Karpis and Fred Hunter.

During **World War II**, the number of FBI agents grew from 600 to more than 5,000. Although the size of the force shrank after 1945, the prestige of the FBI and the power of Hoover were not diminished.

In the turbulent 1960s, Hoover was ordered by President **Lyndon B. Johnson** (see no. 86) to use his power to enforce federal civil-rights laws in the south. Hoover obeyed orders, but simultaneously carried out a personal vendetta against civil-rights leader **Martin Luther King, Jr.** (see no. 96). Hoover's attempts to create additional difficulties for King, in a series of actions under the umbrella term "King Cointelpro," were kept secret during Hoover's lifetime.

He died in 1972, having held power at the FBI through the administrations of nine presidents (five Republicans and four Democrats).

76. Duke Ellington
(1899–1974)

Considered one of America's greatest composers, jazz legend **Edward Kennedy Ellington** was born in Washington, D.C. His father was a White House butler and blueprint maker. Ellington grew up in middle-class circumstances and attended Armstrong High School, where he showed interest in athletics and art as well as music. His elegant dress and manner earned him the nickname, "**Duke**," from fellow classmates. Influenced by the piano performers of that era, such as **James P. Johnson**, he began to substitute for pianist Lester Dishman in Washington, D.C., and in 1913, wrote his first composition, "Soda Fountain Rag."

Ellington married Edna Thompson in 1918; the couple had one son, Mercer.

In 1923, Ellington moved to New York City and joined a five-piece combo called The Washingtonians. He soon became the leader, and between 1923 and 1927 his band performed frequently at the **Hollywood Club** (later called the Kentucky Club). Greater fame arrived in December 1927, when he premiered the **Duke Ellington Orchestra** at the **Cotton Club** in the Harlem section of New York City. In his years at the Cotton Club (1927–1931), Ellington pioneered his "jungle style," which employed trumpet and trombone "growls."

Separated from his wife in 1930, Ellington brought his mother and sister to join him and Mercer in Harlem. Always extremely close to his mother, Ellington was devastated by her death in 1935. His grief led to one of his finest works, "Reminiscing in Tempo."

In 1933, during the height of the **Great Depression**, Ellington took his 14-piece orchestra on an extended tour of England and the European continent. The rave reviews he received prompted Ellington to continue touring. In fact, he maintained a nearly constant stream of appearances for the rest of his life.

Ellington's most creative period was 1930 through 1942, during which he composed "Mood Indigo" (1930), "Sophisticated Lady" (1932), "It Don't Mean a Thing (If It Ain't Got That Swing)"(1932), "In a Sentimental Mood" (1935), and "Cotton Tail" (1940), among many others. His recording of his collaborator **Billy Strayhorn**'s "Take the 'A' Train" (1941) became the orchestra's theme song.

Ellington enlarged his orchestra to 18 musicians during the 1940s, and in 1943, he presented a program called *Black, Brown, and Beige,* a musical history of the African-American experience in America, at Carnegie Hall.

During the 1950s and 60s, Ellington composed and performed a number of extended "suites," as well as the scores for such films as *Anatomy of a Murder* and *Paris Blues.*

Duke Ellington died of cancer in 1974.

Duke Ellington

Perhaps the most gifted speaker in American public life during the 20th century, **Adlai Ewing Stevenson** strove to serve the causes of liberalism and world government. He was the grandson of another Adlai E. Stevenson, who served as vice president during the Cleveland administration from 1893 to 1897. Stevenson graduated from Princeton University (1922) and earned his law degree from Northwestern University (1926).

Stevenson was a prominent member of the **Committee to Defend America** by aiding the Allies prior to America entering **World War II**. He was special assistant to the Secretary of the Navy (1941–1944) and was transferred to the State Department in 1945. He led the U.S. commission that prepared for the opening of the **United Nations** (1945) and was a U.S. delegate to that body (1946 and 1947).

In 1948, he ran in his first political election (the only one he ever won) and became the Democratic governor of Illinois. As such, he was approached by many Democrats who urged him to run for president in 1952. Stevenson declined at first, but accepted a draft by the Democratic convention and ran unsuccessfully against World War II hero **Dwight D. Eisenhower** (see no. 72).

Stevenson defended the Democratic record of outgoing President **Harry S. Truman**, but unlike Truman, who relished a philosophy of "give 'em hell," Stevenson believed in "talking sense" to the American people. However, Stevenson's elegant and involved speeches — which avoided quick and easy solutions to intractable problems — failed to win over the American electorate, giving the victory to Eisenhower by an electoral vote of 442 to 89.

Stevenson ran again in 1956. He sought the nomination actively and campaigned with vigor, but he went down to defeat a second time, receiving only 73 electoral votes. He

Adlai E. Stevenson

sought the Democratic nomination again in 1960, but was beaten by **John F. Kennedy** (see no. 92), who, though he lacked Stevenson's profundity of thought, was equal to Stevenson in wit and public presence.

Stevenson then served as U.S. ambassador to the United Nations (1961–1965) under presidents Kennedy and **Lyndon B. Johnson** (see no. 86). One of his great satisfactions came in 1963 with the approval of the **Nuclear Test Ban Treaty** which banned nuclear testing in the atmosphere. Unfortunately, on key policy issues such as Cuba and relations with the Soviet Union, Stevenson was not as influential as such Cabinet insiders as Secretary of State **Dean Rusk** and Secretary of Defense **Robert McNamara**. Stevenson continued to serve in his post until he died in 1965 of a heart attack.

78. Walt Disney
(1901–1966)

Walter Elias Disney was born in Chicago, Illinois. During his high school years, he took classes at the Chicago Academy of Fine Arts, but never graduated from high school.

Too young to serve as a soldier in **World War I**, Disney became an **American Red Cross** ambulance driver. He and McDonald's founder **Ray Kroc** (see no. 80) were in the same ambulance unit. Returning to the United States, Disney became a commercial artist in Kansas City, working for Ub Iwerks, a pioneer animator.

Disney left the midwest for Los Angeles, California in 1923. He and his brother Roy converted a garage into a studio and created two cartoon series: *Alice in Cartoonland* (1924–1926) and *Oswald the Rabbit* (1926–1928).

It was during a long train trip between New York City and Los Angeles that Disney thought up his most famous cartoon character, **Mickey Mouse**. He and Roy made two silent films that featured Mickey, but it was *Steamboat Willie* (1928), the first sound cartoon, that made the mouse famous. Mickey Mouse rapidly became a household name in America, then an international attraction, and finally a true American cultural totem. After 1927, Disney did very little actual animation; instead he hired a team of cartoon artists to draw the pictures and stories he imagined.

Disney built on his success by releasing *Flowers and Trees* (1932), the first short film made completely in Technicolor. Even more important was *Snow White and the Seven Dwarfs* (1937), the first full-length animated feature, which became an immediate success. Disney followed with *Pinocchio* (1939), *Fantasia* (1940) and *Bambi* (1942).

During **World War II**, Disney's studio made educational films for the government as part of the war effort, many featuring the characters of Mickey Mouse, Donald Duck, Goofy and Pluto.

Disney also produced a series of "true life adventures" films such as *Seal Island* (1948) and *Beaver Valley* (1950), as well as movies with live actors including *Treasure Island* (1950), *Davy Crockett* (1955) and *Mary Poppins* (1964), featuring a relatively unknown Julie Andrews in the title role.

In 1955, Disney opened **Disneyland**, the ultimate theme park of its time which pioneered an industry. Disneyland drew millions of visitors to Anaheim, California each year including such unusual guests as the Soviet Union's premier, Nikita Khruschev.

Disneyland paved the way for the opulent **Walt Disney World** near Orlando, Florida, although, Disney would not see this dream come to fruition during his lifetime.

Walt Disney

Few writers have displayed such a depth of feeling for the land, people of America, and California in particular, as did **John Steinbeck**. Born in Salinas, California, he was one of four children of a county bureaucrat and a schoolteacher mother. He studied sporadically at Stanford University but left without earning a degree.

His work in the sugarbeet fields of California, as a handyman on a ranch and in a fish hatchery all contributed to develop Steinbeck's understanding of the life of everyday Americans during the years of the **Great Depression**. Steinbeck's novel, *Tortilla Flat*, published in 1935 after a dozen publishers had previously rejected it, earned his work a place on American bookshelves.

Steinbeck soon followed *Tortilla Flat* with the three books that marked the peak of his career. *In Dubious Battle* (1936) portrayed an agricultural strike; *Of Mice and Men* (1937) told the painful story of two migrant workers seeking a home in the California countryside; and *The Grapes of Wrath* (1939) expounded on the theme of Oklahoma farmers headed for California in the wake of the **Dust Bowl** of the 1930s. Steinbeck's evocative descriptions of the desperate circumstances of people's lives made him perhaps the greatest artistic realist of his time period. The pain and suffering of millions of Americans was captured in his stirring tales of the continuing search for home, safety and some type of moral redemption.

In 1941, Steinbeck went to Mexico to film a documentary movie and write *The Sea of Cortez*. He worked as a foreign correspondent during **World War II**, and that provided the material for *Bombs Away!* (1942) and *Once There Was a War* (1958). In 1945, he published *Cannery Row*, a strong depiction of the sights and sounds of the sardine industry and canneries in Monterey, California.

John Steinbeck

Steinbeck's major work of the 1950s was his novel, *East of Eden* (1952), based somewhat on the Biblical story of Cain and Abel. In 1961, he published *The Winter of Our Discontent*, an examination of middle-class American values. It is difficult to say which he found more disconcerting, the pain of Americans during the Great Depression or the complacent suburban life depicted in his last novel.

Steinbeck published a travel memoir, *Travels with Charley*, in 1962. That same year he was awarded the Nobel Prize for literature for his body of work. His thrill at receiving the award was tempered by the lack of enthusiasm this honor received from East Coast literary critics.

John Steinbeck died in 1968, recognized as one of America's greatest writers and humanists.

80. Ray Kroc
(1902–1984)

Fast-food industry pioneer **Ray Kroc** was born in Chicago, Illinois. He attended public schools, dropped out at the age of 15, lied about his age and drove an ambulance for the **American Red Cross** during **World War I**. On his return home, Kroc became a jazz pianist and then turned to sales after he married Joan Dobbins in 1922.

Kroc went to work for the Lily-Tulip Cup Company, but at the same time, he was the music director for a pioneer radio station in Chicago. He left both jobs in 1924 and went to Florida where he sold real estate. He lost everything in late 1926 when the Florida real estate boom suddenly went bust. Kroc returned to work for Lily-Tulip and soon became a regional manager of sales for the company.

In 1937, Kroc came across a new invention, a five-spindled milk shake mixer that could blend five different shakes at the same time. He became the exclusive sales agent for the Multimixer machine and started his own company to market the product.

This brought Kroc prosperity, and led him, in 1954, to discover a restaurant in San Bernardino County, California where two brothers, **Dick** and **Mac McDonald**, were using eight of the mixers. Their restaurant sold only hamburgers, French fries and milk shakes using an assembly-line technique that saved time and money. Impressed by the brothers, Kroc entered into an agreement with them to start a chain of drive-in restaurants and the brothers, in turn, would receive one-half of one percent of the gross income.

Kroc opened the first **McDonald's** restaurant in Des Plaines, Illinois on April 15, 1955. He soon sold his Multimixer company and used the profits to accelerate the opening of additional McDonald's restaurants. By 1960, there were 228 restaurants and Kroc bought out the McDonald brothers for $2.7 million the following year. The 2,000th McDonald's opened its doors in mid-1972. (The "Big Mac" sandwich was created in 1968.)

Kroc had streamlined the art of fast food to a science. He selected many of the early restaurant sites by reconnoitering in a helicopter and finding strategic locations, near shopping centers and traffic lights. The restaurants were readily identifiable by their golden arches and the flying of an American flag. Kroc was chairman of the board from 1968 to 1977.

On January 25, 1975, Kroc purchased the San Diego Padres to prevent the baseball club from moving to Washington, D.C. When he died on January 14, 1984, his widow, Joan, succeeded Kroc as owner and chairwoman of the team. The Padres would go on to represent the National League in the World Series later that year.

Ray Kroc

81. Charles Lindbergh
(1902–1974)

Charles Augustus Lindbergh went to the University of Wisconsin to study civil engineering and dropped out of the academic program to enter flying school in Lincoln, Nebraska.

Flying was the rage of the 1920s, and Lindbergh bought an army surplus plane for $500 and tried barnstorming (performing flight demonstrations) for a year. He entered army flying school, graduated first in his class and was commissioned a second lieutenant in 1925.

Lindbergh worked for a time as an airmail pilot. By early 1927, he became fixed on the idea of winning the $25,000 Orteig prize, which was to be awarded to the first person to fly solo from New York City to Paris, France. Lindbergh helped to design the "**Spirit of St. Louis**" plane and, on May 20, 1927, he took off from **Roosevelt Field** on Long Island, New York. He took neither a parachute nor a radio in favor of carrying more fuel, and took only five sandwiches and a quart of water. Lindbergh flew the northern route, over Nova Scotia, Newfoundland and Ireland. He landed at **Le Bourget Airport** in Paris after a 33-hour, 29-minute flight in which he covered 3,610 miles.

The exhausted American stepped out of the plane to be greeted by tremendous cheers from French spectators; in that hour Lindbergh became the most famous private citizen of the United States. He returned in triumph to the United States aboard a navy cruiser sent specifically for that purpose by President **Calvin Coolidge**.

Lindbergh married Anne Spencer Morrow, daughter of the U.S. ambassador to Mexico, in 1929. Their son, Charles A. Lindbergh, Jr., was kidnapped and killed in 1932. The grief of the Lindbergh family, and the outrage on the part of the American public, led to passage in Congress of the "**Lindbergh Law**,"

Charles Lindbergh with *Spirit of St. Louis*

making kidnapping a federal crime.

While on duty in the U.S. Air Corps, Lindbergh became active in the **America First Committee**, which favored a policy of "**Isolationism**" and sought to prevent U.S. entry into **World War II**. Lindbergh had the misfortune to draw the wrath of President **Franklin D. Roosevelt** (see no. 70), who publicly criticized the aviator during a press conference on April 25, 1941. Lindbergh immediately resigned his colonel's commission, a move that confused his supporters and followers.

In actuality, Lindbergh volunteered for service during the war and flew 50 fighter-plane missions over the Pacific as a civilian. He also worked with automaker **Henry Ford** (see no. 61) on the development of B-24 bombers. Lindbergh won the Pulitzer Prize for his book *The Spirit of St. Louis* (1953), and was made a brigadier general in the Air Force Reserve by President **Dwight D. Eisenhower** (see no. 72) in 1954.

The pediatrician who changed the way Americans raised their children, **Benjamin McLane Spock** graduated from Phillips Andover Academy and Yale College (1925). Spock entered medical school and graduated from Columbia University College of Physicians and Surgeons (1929). He also studied at the New York Psychoanalytic Institute for six years.

Spock built a private practice in pediatrics (1933–1944) before serving as a psychiatrist in the navy during **World War II** (1944–1946). He left the navy after rising to the rank of lieutenant commander. During slack periods of his military service, he began writing the book that was to change the lives of millions of Americans. It was first published in 1946 as *The Common Sense Book of Baby and Child Care* and later published under the abbreviated title *Baby and Child Care*.

Spock's work soon began to alter the ways Americans brought up their children. He urged parents to follow common sense and to raise their children with trust, affection and love. Roughly three million copies of the book were sold during the first three years after publication; by 1972 the total number sold had reached 24 million. An entire generation of American parents were exposed to Spock's guidelines, and a great number of parents heeded the advice.

Spock went on to serve at the Mayo Clinic and at the Rochester Child Health Project (1947–1951), the University of Minnesota (1947–1951), the University of Pittsburgh Medical School (1951–1955) and Western Reserve University (1955–1967). He continued to write columns on child care.

In 1962, Spock became co-chairman of the National Committee for a Sane Nuclear Policy. Advertisements soon appeared showing Spock holding children in his arms, with captions that declared he was worried about the future of children due to radiation. His political views became progressively stronger during the 1960s. A prominent member of the National Mobilization Committee to End the War in Vietnam, he played an important role in a number of peace demonstrations.

Because of these activities, Spock was arrested and indicted in 1968 along with William Sloane Coffin, Jr., Marcus Raskin, Mitchell Goodman and William Ferber. A short trial resulted in all but Raskin being found guilty of inciting young people to evade the draft, but a U.S. Court of Appeals ruling reversed the decision in 1969.

Spock, who began his political life as a Republican, switched to the Democratic Party during the **New Deal** reforms of the 1930s and became a convert to socialism as a result of his experiences in the peace movement during the Vietnam War. He wrote *Dr. Spock on Vietnam* (1968) and ran for president in 1972 as the People's Party candidate.

Benjamin Spock

(1904–1967)

The most influential American physicist was **Julius Robert Oppenheimer**. He graduated from New York City's Ethical Culture School (1921) and then from Harvard (1925). He went abroad for his graduate work, studying in Ernest Rutherford's laboratory in Cambridge, England, and then with Max Born at the University of Gottingen in Germany. With Born, he wrote a paper on the quantum theory of molecules, which soon became known as the "**Born-Oppenheimer Method**."

Having earned his Ph.D. at Gottingen, Oppenheimer returned to the United States and took up two simultaneous academic positions at the University of California at Berkeley and the California Institute of Technology (Cal Tech). An inspired teacher and mentor, Oppenheimer laid the groundwork for American pre-eminence in the field of physics by training an entire new generation of American scholars in that field.

During the 1930s, Oppenheimer was drawn to liberal and left-wing causes; he formed a number of important friendships that would later be used as evidence that he was not fully committed to American capitalism and democracy.

However, in June 1942, he joined the secret "**Manhattan Project**," which was engaged in the making of the first American **atomic bomb**. Oppenheimer was made director of the central laboratory at Los Alamos, New Mexico, in 1943. In July 1945, he and a small group of scientists stood by while the first atomic test occurred.

Seeing the radioactive cloud rise to the sky caused a multitude of feelings, some of which Oppenheimer later recalled: "We knew the world would not be the same. A few people laughed, a few people cried. Most people were silent. I remembered the line from the Hindu scripture, the *Bhagavad Gita,* 'I am become

J. Robert Oppenheimer

Death, the destroyer of worlds.' I suppose we all thought that, one way or another."

Exhausted from his work and troubled by the implications of nuclear power, Oppenheimer resigned from his position as director. He served as director of the Institute for Advanced Study at Princeton University from 1947 to 1966, which became the central point for advanced theoretical physics in the world.

As a member of the general advisory commission for the **Atomic Energy Commission** from 1946 to 1952, and the **Science Advisory Commission** from 1951 to 1954, Oppenheimer drew the enmity of leaders in the air force who revealed that some of Oppenheimer's friends were known to be socialists or communists. His security clearance was revoked by President **Dwight D. Eisenhower** (see no. 72) in December 1953.

Oppenheimer had the satisfaction of receiving the **Enrico Fermi Award** in December 1963 before his death from cancer.

84. William Levitt
(1907–1994)

William J. Levitt was born in Brooklyn, New York. He attended New York University for three years but left without earning a degree, eager to find a way to make money.

In 1929, he founded **Levitt & Sons, Inc**. with his father, Abraham, and his younger brother, Alfred. The three men each specialized according to their ability. Alfred designed homes. William concentrated on finances, sales and real estate transactions. Abraham did the landscaping.

The family firm built and sold 600 houses between 1929 and 1933, no small feat in the early years of the **Great Depression**. Then they built **Strathmore-at-Manhasset**, a township of 200 homes (1934) and built 2,000 more houses before the start of **World War II**. When the war began, the family company demonstrated its successful methods by producing 2,350 housing units for the U.S. Navy in 18 months. Following a period of service in the Pacific with the Seabees unit of the navy, William returned home and made plans to meet the housing needs of the approximately eight million Americans who had served in uniform during the war.

Between 1947 and 1951, the Levitts built 17,500 one-family houses on a tract of land (that used to be potato farms) and called it "**Levittown**," a 7.3-square-mile area on New York's Long Island. Using mass-production and mass-construction methods, the workers could assemble as many as 36 houses in one day. Many observers applauded the energy and skill of the company, while crit-ics asserted that the entire process cheapened and even vulgarized what it meant to have a true family home. A second Levittown was built near the Delaware River in Bucks County, Pennsylvania (1951), and a third in nearby New Jersey.

Abraham and Alfred left the company by the mid-1950s, and William Levitt carried his work forward alone. One controversial aspect of his housing was that he explicitly refused to sell housing units to African-Americans. Asserting that as a Jewish-American he had no personal racial prejudice, Levitt insisted that if he did sell to African-Americans he would lose 90 to 95 percent of his white customers.

Levitt sold his company to International Telephone and Telegraph for $492 million in 1968. He was, for a time, one of the wealthiest men in America, but business ventures overseas during the 1970s and 1980s depleted his fortune, and the man who had made housing affordable for millions of people was eventually forced to sell both his yacht and his real estate. He died in New York City, having built approximately 140,000 houses during a career that paved the way for the boom growth of the American suburbs.

Aerial view of Levittown, NY

Edward R. Murrow
(1908–1965)

"This ... is London" were the words that began nearly every **Columbia Broadcasting System** (CBS) radio broadcast sent to the United States during the *blitzkrieg* in 1940, when German bombs rained on London and other British cities. The pause and the intonation were unmistakable; it was **Edward R. Murrow** reporting on the latest news about **World War II**.

He was born in Greensboro, North Carolina and worked at first as a compass man and topographer for timber companies in Washington before he went to college at Stanford University, the University of Washington and Washington State College, where he studied history and speech.

Following graduation in 1930, Murrow served as president of the National Student Federation; in that capacity he visited and reported on conditions at more than 300 American colleges. He then served as assistant director of the Institute for International Education (1932–1933) and secretary of the Emergency Commission for the Aid of Displaced German Scholars (1933–1935).

Murrow joined CBS in 1935, and in 1937 he was made chief of the system's European bureau. He gave the first of his war-related reports in 1938, when Nazi forces entered Vienna. However, it was the German aerial bombardment of southern England in 1940 that truly brought Murrow to prominence, at home and abroad.

At a time when many Americans feared Britain would fall as swiftly as had France to the German war machine, Murrow's crisp, professional reports stood out for their clarity. While he did not seek to encourage false hope, Murrow sent radio transmissions that were authoritative and somehow comforting to the millions of Americans who listened to them. He remained at his London post throughout the war, then returned to the

Edward R. Murrow

United States and briefly worked as a vice president of CBS, in charge of all the news broadcasts, from 1945 to 1947.

Finding that he liked reporting far more than being an executive, Murrow returned to radio to present *Hear It Now*, a weekly radio news digest, and then *See It Now*, a television documentary that, among other things, did the first televised show of a state legislature in action (Arkansas, 1951). He produced and hosted *Person to Person* (1953–1960) and *Small World* (1958–1960). His most important television shows exposed the manipulative tactics of U.S. Senator **Joseph R. McCarthy** (see no. 87); another, called *Harvest of Shame*, exposed the plight of migratory farm workers in the United States. Murrow also served as director of the United States Information Agency (1961–1963).

86. Lyndon Baines Johnson
(1908–1973)

Lyndon Baines Johnson was born on his parents' farm near Johnson City, Texas. In 1934, Johnson married Claudia Taylor, who became known as **Lady Bird Johnson**.

He then ran for elected office for the first time and served in the U.S. House of Representatives (1937–1949). Johnson's time in office was interrupted by military service in **World War II**. He was the first congressman to enlist for service in the war.

In 1948, Johnson won the Democratic nomination for senator. He served in the U.S. Senate from 1949–1961. Johnson thrived in the Senate, becoming minority leader, and then, majority leader after the 1954 congressional elections put the Democrats in the majority. (As with FDR and JFK, Johnson would come to be known by his initials, frequently referred to as LBJ.)

In 1960, Senator **John F. Kennedy** (see no. 92) asked Johnson to run on the Democratic ticket as his vice presidential candidate. The Kennedy-Johnson ticket won, and Johnson became a very active vice president, traveling extensively on behalf of the administration. On November 22, 1963, hours after Kennedy had been assassinated in Dallas, Texas, Johnson was sworn in as the 36th president of the United States aboard Air Force One.

Vowing to continue the policies Kennedy had outlined, Johnson actually surpassed them in a number of ways. His knowledge of congressional and senatorial politics enabled him to work toward a "**Great Society**" free from hunger, fear and racial divisiveness. Landmark legislation such as the **Voting Rights Act** (1965) and the start of **affirmative action** was passed during Johnson's presidency.

In 1964, LBJ had the satisfaction of winning the presidency in his own right, a landslide of more than 60 percent of the vote over Republican challenger **Barry M. Goldwater**.

There was one legacy from the Kennedy years that came to haunt Johnson: U.S. involvement in the **Vietnam War**. Johnson and his top policy advisers believed it was necessary to contain communism in southeast Asia, or other countries might "fall" in a "domino effect." Therefore, the president sent hundreds of thousands of American troops, and committed the air force to bombing raids, which were regarded by many Americans as barbaric in their indiscriminate killing of civilians as well as enemy soldiers. Protests within the United States mounted. Feeling the pressure, Johnson announced on March 31, 1968, that he would not seek another term in office.

LBJ retired to his ranch in Texas, where he wrote his memoirs.

Lyndon Baines Johnson

87. Joseph R. McCarthy
(1908–1957)

Joseph R. McCarthy

The most unusual, some would say sinister, of all American political leaders was **Joseph R. McCarthy**. He studied at Marquette University and graduated with a law degree in 1935. McCarthy became a district judge in 1939 and served as a lieutenant in the Marine Corps. during **World War II**.

McCarthy made an abortive run for the U.S. Senate in 1944 (while still on active duty), but in 1946, won a stunning primary victory over fellow Republican Robert M. LaFollette, Jr. The LaFollette family (father and son) had held the Senate seat for 40 years prior to 1946.

McCarthy defeated his Democratic opponent and went to Washington in 1947, where he joined a host of other new legislators, **Richard M. Nixon** (see no. 89) and **John F. Kennedy** (see no. 92) among them. From the start, McCarthy was abrasive and contentious in Senate debates, and for nearly three years he was regarded as an ineffectual boor by many of his colleagues.

McCarthy stunned his critics and made himself known to the entire nation in 1950 when he announced that he had evidence of 57 known Communists operating in the U.S. State Department. Capitalizing on the pro-found American fear of infiltration by Soviet agents, he vowed to lead a crusade to root out any such elements from the government.

Within weeks, McCarthy obtained more power than almost any other single legislator in Washington. Although both President **Harry S. Truman** and his successor, **Dwight D. Eisenhower** (see no. 72), despised McCarthy, neither spoke out against him, and his fame and power increased in the early years of the decade.

McCarthy won re-election to the Senate in 1952 and was seen by many as the friend of the people, seeking to keep America safe from communism. Overlooked at first were the facts that he had no substantive evidence to back his charges. The height of his power came in 1953 when McCarthy became chairperson of the **Senate Committee on Government Operations** and the permanent subcommittee on investigations.

McCarthy rode high until he took on members of the armed services in the **Army-McCarthy Hearings** (April 22 through June 17, 1954), which were televised. Although at first the American public welcomed his relentless pursuit of the truth, many people soon became disgusted by his outbursts of anger and bullying of witnesses.

When the hearings concluded, polls found McCarthy's favorable rating among the American people had dropped to 34 percent. Emboldened by this, his fellow senators conducted an investigation, and on December 2, 1954, he was publicly censured by the Senate. His career virtually over, McCarthy was largely ignored by the press, his colleagues and the general public. He died of complications caused by cirrhosis of the liver.

A brilliant manipulator of public opinion, McCarthy gave his name to the phenomenon called "**McCarthyism**," referring to unjust and unsubstantiated accusations.

Veterans of the civil rights movement believe their struggle officially received recognition on December 1, 1955. **Rosa Parks**, an African-American woman, refused to yield her seat on a Montgomery, Alabama bus to a white man. City laws reserved the first 10 rows on buses for white people. Parks was sitting in the 11th row. However, African-American passengers were expected to give up their seats to whites when buses filled up. Parks' refusal to comply led to her arrest. She went to jail that night, but was quickly released on a $100 bond.

While working as a seamstress, Parks had joined the Montgomery branch of the **National Association for the Advancement of Colored People** (NAACP) where she served as its secretary from 1943–1956.

When Parks made her decision on December 1, 1955, she was aware of the possibility (but not the certainty) there would be support for her action. Parks was tried by the city of Montgomery on December 5, found guilty of violating the law, and fined $10 and court costs of an additional $4. She refused to pay the fine and appealed the case to the district court. On the day she was tried, 7,000 members of Montgomery's black community came together and formed the **Montgomery Improvement Association**, with the Reverend **Martin Luther King, Jr.** as its first president (see no. 96).

A one-day boycott of the Montgomery bus system was undertaken; seeing how it united most of the black community, the leaders decided to continue the boycott until the segregation laws were changed. For 381 days (December 5, 1955–December 21, 1956), the great majority of African-Americans in Montgomery walked to work rather than use the bus system.

On June 2, 1956, the U.S. district court declared segregation on the buses unconstitutional, and the U.S. Supreme Court upheld the decision of the lower court. A court order was served on Montgomery December 20, 1956, ending the segregation policy and bringing the boycott to a triumphant conclusion.

Rosa Parks lost her job during the boycott and would not find suitable work in Montgomery again. She moved to Detroit, Michigan in 1957 and served as an assistant to U.S. Representative John Conyers in his Detroit office (1965–1988). The "first lady of civil rights" continued her work in the **Southern Christian Leadership Conference**, and in 1987, she established the **Rosa and Ray Parks Institute for Development** for young people.

Rosa Parks

89. Richard M. Nixon
(1913–1994)

One of the most controversial and combative of American presidents, **Richard Milhous Nixon** attended Whittier College (in Orange County, California), where he excelled in history and debate. He went to Duke University Law School and earned his law degree in 1937.

Nixon served in the U.S. Navy during **World War II** then chose to run for public office. He won election to the U.S. House of Representatives in 1946, and four years later, became the youngest person elected to the U.S. Senate.

In 1952, Republican presidential nominee **Dwight D. Eisenhower** (see no. 72) asked Nixon to run for vice president. Nixon agreed and served as vice president from 1953 to 1961.

In 1960, Nixon ran for the presidency. Skilled in debate, he accepted the challenge of Democratic nominee Senator **John F. Kennedy** (see no. 92) to engage in three televised debates. To television viewers, Nixon seemed ill at ease in comparison to Kennedy.

The debates made the difference in an extremely close election, which Nixon lost. A subsequent loss in his 1962 race for governor of California led Nixon to tell the press, "You won't have Nixon to kick around any more."

Nixon made a remarkable comeback in 1968, winning the presidency in a close election over Democrat **Hubert H. Humphrey**. He won re-election by a landslide in 1972 and appeared to be on the way to making his place in history. He pulled the majority of American troops out of **Vietnam**, was the first American president to visit China, and stood firm in a confrontation with the Soviets during the **Arab-Israeli War** of 1973.

Unfortunately, Nixon lost all credibility over the issue of "**Watergate**," a 1972 burglary of the Democratic national political headquarters by men working for the president.

Richard M. Nixon

Not only did Nixon sanction the break-in, he made a massive attempt to cover up his complicity.

Making matters worse, Nixon tape recorded thousands of conversations held in the Oval Office. When these tapes were subpoenaed by the Senate investigations committee, an extremely unappealing portrait of the president emerged — it was clear Nixon was dishonest, paranoid and vindictive. He was forced to resign the presidency, and did on August 9, 1974 — the only president to have done so in American history.

Nixon retired to California and soon received a full, unconditional pardon for any wrongs he might have committed by his successor and former vice president, **Gerald R. Ford**.

Although he labored to rebuild his reputation and did emerge as something of an elder statesman in later years, Nixon could not reverse the standing the Watergate crisis had created. Nixon remains the epitome of an American political leader who had fallen from grace.

90. Thomas J. Watson, Jr.
(1914–1993)

Born in Dayton, Ohio, **Thomas J. Watson, Jr.**, was the oldest son of Thomas Watson, Sr., who became president of the Computing-Tabulating-Recording Company in the same year as his son's birth. The young Watson attended private schools and graduated from Brown University (1937), where, he later admitted, he studied little and spent much of his time engrossed with airplanes.

In 1937, Watson went to work as a junior salesman for his father's company, which the senior Watson had renamed **International Business Machines (IBM)** in 1924. Thomas, Jr. was given the Wall Street area, a particularly tough district, as his first sales territory. In his early years with the company, Watson sold two-and-a-half times as many machines within his territory as had been sold there before by more experienced salespeople. This, his baptism by fire at IBM, was the launching pad for his future success.

Watson joined the U.S. Air Force at the start of **World War II**. Commissioned a second lieutenant, he was one of the first Americans to fly the "**Lend-Lease**" route between Alaska and Russia. He left the Air Force in 1946 as a lieutenant colonel with more than 2,000 hours of recorded flight time.

Watson returned to IBM in 1946 and rapidly ascended the company hierarchy. In January 1952, he became president of IBM, while his father became chairman of the board of directors.

Watson saw the great potential that existed in the new field of office automation. He envisioned and carried out a restructuring program that changed the emphasis at IBM from electromechanical calculators to electronic computers. During Watson's years as president (1952–1971), IBM beat out top rivals **Remington Rand**, **Honeywell** and **General Electric**, positioning itself as the main supplier for **mainframe computers**.

At the same time, the IBM company ethic — which included three-piece suits, a strict code of conduct, and worker loyalty to the company — became the standard many other American companies began to strive for. The conservative attitude that pervaded much of American corporate life during the 1950s and 1960s has often been attributed to the standard set by IBM during Watson's tenure.

Watson retired from the company in 1971. An outspoken liberal Democrat throughout his adult life, he served as U.S. ambassador to the Soviet Union during part of the Carter administration (1979–1981). He lived long enough to witness the decline of IBM's position as the personal computers of the 1980s replaced the former mainframe computers IBM had specialized in. *Fortune* magazine labeled Watson "the greatest capitalist who ever lived."

Thomas J. Watson, Jr. and Sr.

91. Jonas Salk
(1914–1995)

Jonas Edward Salk earned his bachelor of science degree from the College of the City of New York in 1934. He continued his medical studies and earned his M.D. from the New York University College of Medicine in 1939.

Salk underwent a period of residency training at Mount Sinai Hospital from 1940–1942. He then went to the University of Michigan on a special fellowship for the study of the **influenza virus**. Working with Dr. **Thomas Francis**, **Jr.**, Salk developed commercial vaccines intended to battle influenza (which killed some 570,000 Americans in the great epidemic of 1918–1919).

Salk continued at the University of Pittsburgh in 1947, where he was made a research professor of bacteriology and director of the Virus Research Laboratory. It was there that he developed his interest in finding a preventive for **poliomyelitis** (polio) which had affected thousands of Americans, including President **Franklin D. Roosevelt** (see no. 70).

Salk undertook a three-year study of the "typing" of the polio virus. He and his team of researchers found that polio was caused by one of three strains of the virus (labeled I, II and III) and that any potential preventive vaccine would have to be potent against all three types. Salk experimented in the early 1950s with monkeys and humans, and in 1953, he announced he had found a potential cure for the virus. His full prescription, released to the press in 1954, called for the Mahoney strain (Type I), MEF-1 strain (Type II), and the Saukett strain (Type III). The timing of Salk's announcement was especially significant, since an outbreak of polio in 1952 had killed 3,300 of the 57,626 Americans stricken by the epidemic.

Salk tested his serum on 100 adults and children — including himself, his wife and children.

Jonas Salk

By 1954, the U.S. government was ready to use Salk's vaccine. Millions of children were given three injections with serum that had been checked for safety by pharmaceutical makers and the National Institutes of Health. Salk's preventive serum proved remarkably effective. However, it remained the standard treatment for only seven years, and by 1961, the stronger oral vaccine of Albert Sabin had replaced Salk's.

Salk went on to found and direct the **Salk Institute for Biological Studies** (1963) and served on the board of directors of the **Immune Research Corporation**. The doctor also wrote *Man Unfolding* (1972) and *Anatomy of Reality: Merging of Intuition and Reason* (1983). During the last years of his life, Salk worked trying to find an agent that would prevent HIV from turning into full-blown AIDS.

Born in Boston, Massachusetts, **John Fitzgerald Kennedy** was the son of **Joseph P. Kennedy**, a banker and U.S. ambassador to Britain, and **Rose Fitzgerald**, daughter of a prominent Irish-American politician in Boston. A highy intelligent and sometimes inscrutable individual, Kennedy projected a charm, wit and charisma previously unseen in American politics. The idealism he promoted during his brief time in office gave birth to an exciting time of possibility in the early 1960s.

He entered politics gingerly. Experienced politicians who tutored him said he was "aggressively shy," but he won a seat in the U.S. House of Representatives in 1946, and in 1952, he defeated prominent Republican **Henry Cabot Lodge** for a place in the U.S. Senate.

Kennedy married **Jacqueline Bouvier** in 1953. The handsome young couple became known throughout Washington for their social grace.

Kennedy ran for and won the Democratic presidential nomination in 1960 at age 43. He defied the experts who said a Catholic could never become president by defeating Republican **Richard M. Nixon** (see no. 89) in an extremely close election. He became the youngest man ever elected to the presidency.

Kennedy showed a dynamic flair for action during his time in office. He brought to Washington learned professors and professionals from top universities and businesses to help guide public policy. He initiated programs such as the **Peace Corps** and the **Alliance for Progress** to help bring democracy to developing nations.

On a personal level, he and his wife made

John F. Kennedy

the White House into a center for high culture. Together, the Kennedys and their young children (Caroline and John, Jr.) seemed to elevate public life to a higher level.

Kennedy faced several crises in foreign affairs during his presidency. Soon after taking office, Kennedy admitted responsibilty for a failed CIA-backed plot to overthrow Cuban leader Fidel Castro. His administration was forced to stand by helplessly in August 1961, when the Soviet Union erected a wall cutting off East Berlin from the democratic West.

By far the most serious crisis occurred in October 1962, when the United States discovered that the Soviets had installed offensive nuclear missiles in Cuba, only ninety miles from U.S. shores. After conferring with his top advisors, Kennedy ordered a naval quarantine of Cuba and demanded that Soviet leader Nikita Krushchev remove the missiles. Tense negotiations took place over several days, and the entire world watched fearfully as both superpowers stood on the edge of a nuclear confrontation. The standoff ended peacefully when the Soviets agreed to remove the missiles in return for a U.S. pledge not to invade Cuba.

Kennedy was in the early stages of planning for his 1964 re-election campaign when he traveled to Dallas, Texas on November 22, 1963. While riding in a motorcade, he was assassinated by **Lee Harvey Oswald**, an ex-U.S marine turned Communist.

Many Americans believed Oswald, who himself was killed two days after Kennedy, was part of a large conspiracy. However, the **Warren Commission** that investigated the events said that Oswald had acted alone.

93. Jackie Robinson
(1919–1972)

One of the greatest natural athletes ever to play a professional sport, **Jack Roosevelt Robinson** was born near Cairo, Georgia in 1919. Robinson attended Pasadena Junior College and won an athletic scholarship to the University of California at Los Angeles. At UCLA, he played four major sports — football, baseball, basketball and track. In 1938, he led the nation in collegiate punt returns. Robinson was drafted into the Army in 1942, and served as a second lieutenant during **World War II**.

In 1945, Robinson signed a contract to play baseball with the **Kansas City Monarchs**, an African-American team within the **Negro American Baseball League**. His remarkable talent brought him to the attention of **Branch Rickey**, president of the **Brooklyn Dodgers**. Rickey was looking for a talented black ballplayer to integrate the major leagues and break baseball's color barrier. He met with Robinson and signed him to a contract with the Montreal Royals, Brooklyn's top minor league club.

After an outstanding season with Montreal, Rickey brought Robinson up to the majors for the 1947 season. Rickey warned him of the abuse he would be subjected to as the first African-American to play major league baseball; undaunted, Robinson wanted to take on the challenge. During his first year, Robinson was constantly subjected to taunts, threats, and insults from fans, opposing players, and even some of his own teammates.

A less determined athlete might well have walked away from the abuse. However, Robinson was relentless in his pursuit of athletic excellence and his resolve to resist racial prejudice. He had an outstanding first season, and shocked many critics by winning **Rookie of the Year** honors. Robinson played his entire baseball career with the Dodgers. His peak year came in 1949, when he batted .342, stole 37 bases and was named **Most Valuable Player** of the National League. A threat as both a slugger and a bunter, he was an electrifying base stealer who often rattled opposing pitchers into making mistakes. During his ten seasons with the Dodgers, the club won six pennants and one World Series, and Robinson had a career batting average of .311.

Robinson retired from baseball in 1956 to pursue other interests, but his historic undertaking opened the way for hundreds of black and Latin American ballplayers to follow in his footsteps. Jackie Robinson was elected to the **Baseball Hall of Fame** in 1962.

Jackie Robinson

Leading a secure, middle-class American life was no guarantee of happiness, as **Betty Friedan** found out in her early forties. Born Betty Naomi Goldstein in Peoria, Illinois, she was the oldest of three children in a Jewish family. She went to Smith College in Northampton, Massachusetts where she underwent a tremendous personal and intellectual growth. Having graduated in 1942, she went on to do a year of graduate work at the University of California at Berkeley, then returned to the East Coast to Greenwich Village in New York City.

After a short period of bohemian living in New York, she married Carl Friedan, who later became an advertising executive. The couple had three children and moved to a series of progressively finer homes until they lived in an 11-room house overlooking the Hudson River. Surely the Friedans had arrived in life!

However, Betty felt increasingly lonely, restless and dissatisfied. She conducted an extensive survey of her former college classmates and found that many of them also felt that something was missing in their lives. Giving voice to her feelings, Friedan wrote *The Feminine Mystique,* published in 1963. The "mystique," Friedan explained, was a siren call that informed women the only productive life available to them was the role of wife and mother. Rejecting that view, she declared, was the only avenue to freedom for many women.

The book took, selling hundreds of thousands of copies. It went through 15 printings in paperback and was translated into many different languages.

Convinced she needed to do more than write, Friedan founded and served as the first president of the **National Organization for Women** (NOW). Declaring that women had an inalienable right to abortion on demand,

Betty Friedan

24-hour child-care services and equal opportunity in jobs and education, Friedan organized a nationwide women's strike on August 26, 1970 —the 50th anniversary of the passage of the 19th Amendment to the Constitution guaranteeing a woman's right to vote.

Friedan stepped down from the presidency of NOW in 1970. She lobbied hard for the **Equal Rights Amendment**, which failed to win approval in enough states within the time allotted for such legislation to become law. She continued her writing, coming out with *The Second Stage* (1981) and *The Fountain of Age* (1993). Friedan had kindled a movement that burned brightly as women of all social classes began to question their roles in a society that traditionally has denied them equal status and equal opportunities.

95. Malcolm X
(1925–1965)

The most outspoken civil rights leader of the 1960s, **Malcolm Little** was born in Omaha, Nebraska, the seventh of 11 children to a Baptist minister.

Malcolm drifted to Boston, Massachusetts and then to Harlem in New York City, where he took to drug-running, burglary and other crimes. Arrested in Boston in 1946, he was sentenced to 10 years in prison for burglary and larceny. It was in prison, however, that he underwent the first metamorphosis of his life and career.

Introduced to the teachings of **Elijah Muhammad**, Malcolm accepted as literal truth the belief that the original human beings had been black, that Allah had allowed 6,000 years of rule by a race of "white devils," and that Black Muslims would soon establish a separate country where they would dwell in separateness and peace. Upon his parole in 1952, Malcolm Little changed his name to **Malcolm X** (he rejected what he called the "slave name" Little) and became one of the chief evangelical leaders of the **Nation of Islam**. Malcolm X founded new mosques throughout the country and raised the active membership of the Nation of Islam to more than 10,000.

The early 1960s were a time of turmoil in the United States, and Malcolm X came to represent the most extreme elements in the African-American community. Rejecting the peaceful solutions sought by **Martin Luther King, Jr.** (see no. 96), Malcolm X made dramatic speeches that thrilled many of his black listeners and dismayed and angered many white Americans.

His most inopportune remark concerned the assassination of President **John F. Kennedy** (see no. 92); Malcolm X said it was only natural, that it showed the "chickens [of violence and hate] coming home to roost." Elijah Muhammad silenced Malcolm X in the

Malcolm X

wake of controversy following the statement, and in March 1964, Malcolm X left the Nation of Islam. He soon started the **Muslim Mosque** and the **Organization of Afro-American Unity** (1964).

Malcolm X made a *hajj* (pilgrimage) to the Saudi Arabian city of Mecca. Through his talks with Muslims in the wider world, he came to reject the teachings of Elijah Muhammad and to embrace the possibility he might work more peacefully for racial equality in the future.

Upon his return to the United States, Malcolm X formally denounced Elijah Muhammad and the extreme separatism of the Nation of Islam. On February 21, 1965, Malcolm X was shot and killed as he was about to begin a speech at the Audubon Ballroom in New York. Three Black Muslims were tried and found guilty of the murder.

96. Martin Luther King, Jr
(1929–1968)

He was born Michael L. King in Atlanta, Georgia, the son and grandson of Baptist African-American ministers. The father changed his own name and that of his son to *Martin* Luther King in order to honor Martin Luther, the hero of the Protestant Reformation in Germany. **Martin Luther King, Jr.** grew up in the midst of racial prejudice and segregation practiced in the south to become the single most important spokesperson and spiritual leader in the cause of African-American civil rights.

King graduated from Morehouse College in 1948 and from Crozer Theological Seminary in 1951. He earned a Ph.D. at Boston University in 1955.

King became the pastor of Dexter Avenue Baptist Church in Montgomery, Alabama. The furor over civil rights that began when **Rosa Parks** (see no. 88) refused to yield her seat on a bus in 1955 led to a year-long boycott of all the buses in Montgomery; the boycott was led by King.

Continuing to develop and grow as a leader, he became president of the **Southern Christian Leadership Conference** in 1957, the same year he and his wife traveled to Ghana and India. King was inspired by the philosophy and actions of **Mohandas Gandhi** of India; joining Gandhi's nonviolent philosophy with the philosophy of **Henry David Thoreau** (as shown in Thoreau's essay on civil disobedience) became the goal King would devote the rest of his life to achieving.

King led and organized nearly every major African-American protest in the south. He began with demonstrations in Albany, Georgia (1961–1962) and continued with others in Birmingham, Alabama (1963), where King wrote his remarkable "**Letter from Birmingham Jail**." He moved to St. Augustine, Florida (1964) and then faced one of his toughest tests in Selma, Alabama.

During these protests, King was arrested and jailed several times; he also endured stoning by crowds and secret surveillance by the FBI.

His tremendous resolve for peace led to one of the greatest moments for the civil rights movement when, on August 28, 1963, he delivered his "**I Have a Dream**" speech, in front of the Lincoln Memorial in Washington, D.C.

By 1967, King became slightly more aggressive in his tactics. Some scholars speculate that he was becoming a true populist leader.

King went to Memphis, Tennessee in the spring of 1968 to show support for striking city workers there. He was shot and killed as he stood on a hotel balcony; **James Earl Ray** pleaded guilty to the murder and was sentenced to 99 years in prison (where he died in 1998).

Martin Luther King, Jr.

The first human being ever to walk on the moon was **Neil Alden Armstrong**. He built model planes from an early age and started to take flying lessons at 14; he earned his pilot's license on his 16th birthday.

Armstrong studied at Purdue University before entering the Air Force in 1949. He flew 78 combat missions and was shot down once during the **Korean War**. He returned to Purdue and earned his bachelor of science degree in 1955. He became a civilian test pilot for the **National Advisory Committee for Aeronautics** and continued in that capacity after it was renamed the **National Aeronautics and Space Administration** (NASA) in 1958. Armstrong logged some 1,100 hours in test flights by 1962, when he volunteered for and was accepted into the **astronaut** program.

During the 1960s, the United States and Soviet Union were locked in competition to see which nation would be the first to fly in space. Armstrong contributed to U.S. efforts by effecting the first manual space-docking maneuver in 1966.

His true hour of glory, however, was yet to come, and in 1969 it was announced that Armstrong would head the three-person crew (**Edwin E. Aldrin, Jr.**, and **Michael Collins** were the other two) of **Apollo 11**. On July 16, 1969, the three men blasted off from **Cape Kennedy**, Florida. By July 19, they had reached lunar orbit, and the next day, at 4:47 P.M. Eastern Standard Time the lunar module *Eagle* touched down on the surface of the moon.

After a wait of six-and-a-half hours, Armstrong opened the hatch door and stepped out onto the surface of the moon. As he gained his footing, Armstrong (who was being watched by millions of observers on television) uttered the words that were to symbolize the Apollo 11 mission: "That's one

Neil Armstrong

small step for a man, one giant leap for mankind." Armstrong was joined by Aldrin 19 minutes later; Collins was orbiting the moon in the command module *Columbia*.

The two astronauts spent a total of 21 hours on the moon, planting an American flag and gathering samples. They left the moon and successfully rendezvoused with *Columbia*. The reunited crew began its journey home, and at 12:50 P.M. Eastern Standard Time on July 24 they parachuted to safety in the Pacific Ocean. They were swiftly picked up by the *USS Hornet* for medical tests and evaluation before heading home.

Armstrong remained with NASA until 1971, when he left in order to teach engineering at the University of Cincinnati, a position he held until 1979. He then moved on to become the chairperson of CTA, Incorporated, a computer-systems company.

98. Elvis Presley
(1935–1977)

Simply known as "The King," for his ever-lasting impression on the musical genre, **rock 'n' roll**, **Elvis Aron Presley** was born in Tupelo, Mississippi. He was inspired from an early age by the gospel singing in the local Pentacostal church.

Popular music history was made in July 1954, when Presley sang for **Sam Phillips**, owner of **Sun Records** in Memphis. As Bill Black on bass and Scotty Moore on guitar joined Presley, the trio improvised on "Blue Moon of Kentucky" and "That's All Right (Mama)." Phillips saw enormous potential in Presley's remarkable voice.

Phillips sold Presley's contract to RCA Records and by the end of 1956, Elvis topped the *Billboard* magazine music charts five times with "Heartbreak Hotel," "I Want You, I Need You, I Love You," "Don't Be Cruel," "Hound Dog" and "Love Me Tender." Presley's music electrified American youth and horrified their parents. His presence was so overwhelming, the producers of *The Ed Sullivan Show* (January 6, 1957) only filmed him from the waist up — Elvis' pelvic gyrations were considered too provocative for live television.

Presley went to Hollywood and he starred in some 27 formula films during the 1960s. While he made a good deal of money, his lack of acting skill was painfully evident. It would have seemed his recording career had taken a back seat, yet 11 of Presley's soundtrack albums reached the top 10. *G.I. Blues* was number one on *Billboard*'s top 100 album chart for 10 weeks and remained on the chart for 111 weeks! *Blue Hawaii* was number one for 20 weeks!

On December 3, 1968, Presley made a musical comeback with his television special, *Elvis*. He broke the top 20 for the first time in three years with "If I Can Dream," which was followed by "In The Ghetto," "Suspicious Minds" and "The Wonder of You."

He signed an exclusive contract with the International Hotel in Las Vegas, Nevada. Between 1970 and his death seven years later, he gave 1,126 concert performances. His 1973 concert, and subsequent album, *Aloha From Hawaii*, set a popular music milestone when the television special was broadcast live and beamed by satellite world-wide.

Elvis' death from heart failure (he was found dead on the bathroom floor of his mansion, **Graceland**, in Memphis) has not silenced the music. In a span of 20 years, RCA Records released 42 albums since Presley's death.

Statistically, Elvis holds the record for most top 40 hits (107), most top 10 hits (38) and most weeks at number one on the charts (80). Additionally, Elvis had 18 number one singles.

Elvis Presley

Steve Jobs & Stephen Wozniak
(1955-) & (1950-)

In the summer of 1971, **Steve Jobs** was working at Hewlett-Packard, where he met **Stephen Wozniak**. That meeting was the beginning of a friendship and business relationship that would have a profound effect on technology and the computer industry.

Jobs worked as a designer of video games for the Atari company from 1974 to 1975. He and Wozniak co-founded **Apple Company, Inc.** in 1975. The pair bought a $25 microprocessor and set to the task of adaptation. Working together in the Jobs family garage, they designed the Apple I computer, a user-friendly alternative to the larger computers produced by International Business Machines (IBM). Wozniak did most of the actual production work; Jobs stood by and clarified what an extraordinary change this new computer represented.

Prior to 1975, nearly all computers were gargantuan machines connected by large numbers of vacuum tubes. Jobs and Wozniak changed that concept by creating **Apple I**, which could be used by any person diligent and persistent enough to read the computer manual's directions.

Jobs and Wozniak went on to develop the elegant **Apple II** (1977), which sold for $1,350, and then **Lisa**, which stands for **Local Integrated Software Architecture**. Lisa was the first of a new generation of personal computers aimed at executives and their employees.

The Apple company had earnings of $139 million in its first three years (1975–1978), and by 1983 the company had 4,700 employees and $983 million in sales orders. The company hit its greatest success in 1984 with the production of the **Macintosh** computer, Jobs' special design, which was exciting and easy to use for new computer owners.

Jobs and Wozniak's partnership hit rocky times as their fame and wealth increased.

Steve Jobs & Steve Wozniak

Wozniak took two years off after he suffered injuries in a plane crash. He returned to the company in 1983 and left again in 1985 after a series of disagreements with Jobs. Wozniak went on to found a new company, **MBF**, in order to explore future possibilities for electronics.

Jobs resigned from Apple (1985) after losing a power struggle with president John Sculley. Jobs went on to found a new company, **NeXT, Inc.**, and in 1988, unveiled the NeXT computer system, intended to make computer use even easier. In 1997, Jobs agreed to return to Apple to head the board until a new president was selected. He was crucial to revitalizing Apple's image through product refinement and a new ad campaign.

Jobs and Wozniak had taken computers out of their secluded status in business and government and brought them to a mass market of millions of consumers eager to stay current with the computer revolution.

100. Bill Gates
(1955-)

Like **John D. Rockefeller** (see no. 51), **Henry Ford** (see no. 61) and other great entrepreneurs, **Bill Gates** created a need for a series of products to simplify computer use and demonstrated the ability to turn it into a great fortune. Born in Seattle to an upper-middle-class family, William H. Gates graduated from high school in 1973. He went to Harvard University, but found he was more interested in working with his close friend Paul Allen on various electronic projects. Gates dropped out of Harvard in 1975.

He and Allen moved to Albuquerque, New Mexico and established a partnership called **Microsoft**. The computer pair enjoyed success with **BASIC**, a computer language that could run in the tiny memory banks of microcomputers.

In 1977, the Tandy Corporation, well known for its popular line of electronic goods, hired Microsoft to develop software for its computers. Gates moved the firm to Bellevue, Washington, near Seattle, and by 1980, he was approached by International Business Machines (IBM) to produce software. Gates made the Microsoft Disk Operating System (**MS-DOS**) and sold it to IBM. By 1983, 40 percent of all personal computers in America were running software made by Microsoft.

Gates moved his company again, to nearby Redmond, Washington in 1986, the same year that his company went public on the stock market. The stock was originally sold at $21 per share. By March 1987, Microsoft's rise in price to $90.75 had made Gates a billionaire at the age of 32. No other American inventor or businessman has ever accumulated so much wealth so quickly.

Seemingly not content with his phenomenal success, in 1985 Gates went on to produce **Windows 3.0**, a system that relied on visual on-screen symbols and a hand-operated "mouse" instead of typed commands. Gates continued to dominate the cutting edge of computer development, and by 1995, his newest release for the Windows system, **Windows 95**, grabbed a firm hold on the imagination of American teachers, business people and the public at large. In 1995, Gates wrote *The Road Ahead*, which extolled the virtues of a digitized economy.

In the late 1990s, Microsoft was hit by a number of federal and state lawsuits alleging that the company engaged in monopolistic practices. In 2001, a federal judge ordered a breakup of the company, but his ruling was overturned on appeal. Over the next several years, Microsoft reached a number of out-of-court settlements regarding lawsuits that claimed the company's installation of Windows in PCs made by other companies violated antitrust statutes.

Bill Gates

107

TRIVIA QUIZ & PROJECTS

Test your knowledge and challenge your friends with the following questions. The answers can be found in the biographies noted.

1. Who was televised from the waist up in 1957 due to controversy?(see no. 98)
2. Twenty-two miles from Mount Rushmore stands a 563-foot-high statue of this American. Who is it? (see no. 53)
3. Who organized the American Association of the Red Cross? (see no. 43)
4. Which two men died on the same day, exactly 50 years after the signing of the Declaration of Independence? (see nos. 4 and 8)
5. What was the "Great White Fleet"? (see no. 58)
6. What stopped Tecumseh from marrying Rebecca Galloway? (see no. 18)
7. What was the Multimixer and why was it significant? (see no. 80)
8. What event haunted Lyndon Johnson's presidency, causing him not to seek another term in office? (see no. 86)
9. Who walked all the way from Indiana to the Gulf of Mexico? (see no. 50)
10. The Liberty Bell in Philadelphia cracked while ringing for whose funeral? (see no. 11)
11. What is the only major American religious denomination to be founded by a woman? Who was its founder? (see no. 42)
12. Who was known as the "Prince of Humbugs" and the "Children's Friend"? (see no. 35)
13. Whom did *Fortune* magazine refer to as "the greatest capitalist of all time"? (see no. 90)
14. Some of the Americans in this book are known for having spoken especially memorable phrases. Identify who said the following:
    A. "All men are created equal." (see no. 8)
    B. "There is properly no history; only biography." (see no. 32)
    C. "We knew the world would not be the same. A few people laughed, a few people cried. Most people were silent." (see no. 83)
    D. "That's one small step for a man, one giant leap for mankind." (see no. 97)
    E. "Give me liberty or give me death." (see no. 6)
    F. "Cast down your bucket where you are." (see no. 56)
    G. "I cannot promise to obey a law I do not respect." (see no. 66)
    H. "Failure is impossible." (see no. 41)
    I. "I leave this rule for others when I'm dead: Be always sure you're right — then go ahead." (see no. 24)
    J. "There! I guess King George will be able to read that!" (see no. 7)
    K. "So, you're the little woman who wrote the book that made this great war!" (see no. 36)

Suggested Projects

1. In 1979, Susan B. Anthony's image was put on a dollar coin in honor of her achievements. Select someone else from this book who you would commemorate by putting their likeness on a coin and write about why you chose that person.

2. Several people in this book were assassinated before they had the opportunity to follow through with their visions. For example, the deaths of Abraham Lincoln, Martin Luther King, Jr., Malcolm X, and John F. Kennedy left a tremendous void in the spirit of America. Describe how the country might have been different had they lived.

Index

Index

Index

Index